CW00503342

PORTSDOWN
PANORAMA

PORTSDOWN PANORAMA

Anthony Triggs

HALSGROVE

First published in Great Britain in 2005

British Library Cataloguing-in-Publication Data
A CIP record for this title is available from the British Library

ISBN 1 84114 477 0

HALSGROVE
Halsgrove House
Lower Moor Way
Tiverton, Devon EX16 6SS
Tel: 01884 243242
Fax: 01884 243325
email: sales@halsgrove.com
website: www.halsgrove.com

Printed and bound in Great Britain by The Cromwell Press, Trowbridge

ACKNOWLEDGEMENTS

Firstly I would like to thank my publisher, Steven Pugsley, and all the staff at Halsgrove for their help. I must also say thank-you to Keely, Lisa and Ray of *The News* library; Alan King and the most helpful staff at the Local Studies Department of the Norrish Central Library, Portsmouth; Brian Goadsby; Bruce Oliver; Andrew Perrin; Peter Rogers; Bob Hunt; Bob Irwin of J.A. Hewes photographers; Maggie and Chris Ballard; Russell Fox; Wendy Bowen of H.C.C. Museums Service, John Sadden; Lucy Pringle; Mark Jenkinson; Terry Luff and Diane Bourne of Portsmouth Water; Philip Magrath; Geoff Salter, and last – but certainly not least – my wife Sue, who suggested this book and whose unfailing support and encouragement is always there.

There is a great deal more to learn about Portsdown Hill, and there is one important site to visit. This is not a geographical site, but the fascinating website operated by Bob Hunt. As the site's address suggests, Bob covers a great deal of detail of what lies beneath the chalk of the hill as well as a lot of above-ground information. Bob's site can be found at www.portsdown-tunnels.org.uk

For more information on the crop circle phenomenon I commend you to Lucy Pringle's website. Whatever your beliefs on these strange appearances, Lucy's pictures will surely provide food for thought – try www.lucypringle.co.uk

The Author

Anthony Triggs is the author of thirteen previous books about the history of the Portsmouth area. He is a retired *News* journalist and he and his wife Sue live at Portchester.

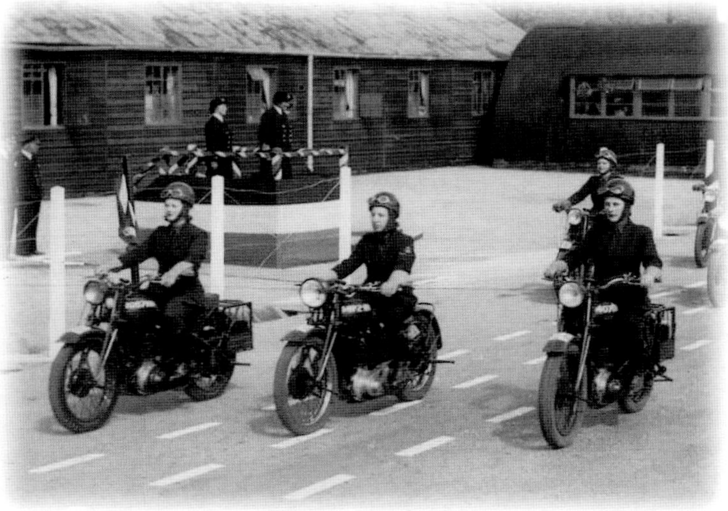

INTRODUCTION

The huge chalk ridge of Portsdown Hill lies like a sleeping giant north of Portsmouth. It can be seen from most parts of the city, but even today, many Portmuthians have never walked on its downs, and many have driven along its ridge but have never stopped to savour what can be seen around them.

The name of Portsdown goes back as far as 1086 when the ridge was known as Portesdone, the last part of the word coming from the Old English *dun*, meaning hill. The history of the hill, however, goes back more than 60 million years when the chalk – which is almost pure calcium carbonate – was formed in marine waters when the calcite shells and skeletons of microscopic organisms fell to the seabed and hardened. Flints, which are also abundant, were formed by colonies of different organisms which produced nodules of the harder substance.

Continental drift played its part in later ages and pushed the chalk up to form the ridge we now know. Early man was attracted by the abundance of the flints, which for thousands of years, they used to make axe-heads, arrowheads and other simple tools. The chalk ridges formed natural trackways, and the elevation provided defensive views of the dense lowland plains below.

Early man also left his mark on Portsdown with a number of barrows, or burial mounds, such as Gob's Barrow, Bevis's Grave, and others along the ridge.

Throughout the Middle Ages and right until recent times sheep farmers tended the flocks on the slopes, which led to the grass remaining short. However, in the '30s and '40s sheep farming ceased and the rabbit population was devastated by myxomatosis, consequently the more coarse grasses flourished and shrubs and bushes began to appear, leading to the present-day appearance of the hill slopes.

Today much of the hill is designated as a Site of Special Scientific Interest, in order to preserve the wonderful selection of wildlife, plants and insects that are to be found on its slopes. Even cattle have been re-introduced.

Chalk cutting over the centuries to provide lime and flints for building has resulted in the south face of the hill being scarred with the huge white pits, which were camouflaged during the war to stop them being used as navigation aids by enemy pilots.

The hill has always provided a defensive position, from the time of early man to Victorian times, when the line of huge forts was built. In the 1850s the threat of a French attack was an

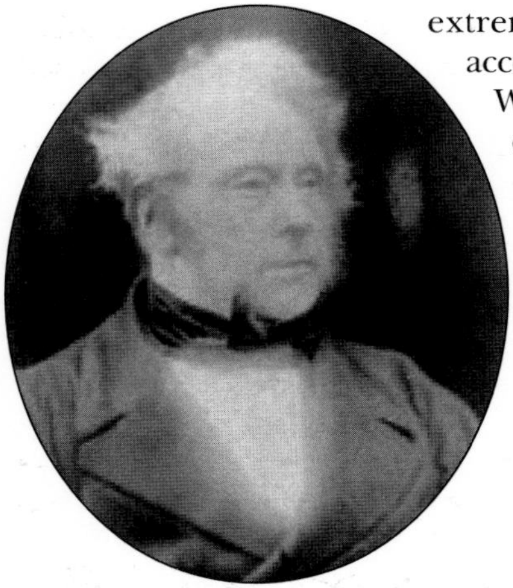

Lord Palmerston.

extremely real one, but it was exacerbated when the British army accepted the Armstrong rifled breech-loading gun into service. With its long range, improved accuracy and greater firepower it caused the government to reconsider British defences. If the French landed on our shores with similar weapons it was thought they could reach Portsdown from the north and bombard the dockyard with devastating results. The Prime Minister, Lord Palmerston, called for a Royal Commission to examine the problem of defence, and as a result the plan for a line of forts along the Portsdown ridge was formulated.

The forts were designed to resist attack from the north, so the views seen from the modern-day road are actually the rear of the buildings.

The five major works were Fort Wallington, Fort Nelson, Fort Southwick, Fort Widley and Fort Purbrook. Three smaller works were also planned – Crookhorn Redoubt, Farlington Redoubt, and Langstone Redoubt. Crookhorn had been demolished by 1876, Langstone was never built, and Farlington was only partly finished, remaining until the 1970s, when it was demolished and is now an industrial site.

But by the time the forts were completed the French threat had receded and the forts were never used, leading to them being called Palmerston's Folly.

Fort Wallington was sold and the site is now an industrial estate; Fort Nelson is under the control of Royal Armouries and is a superb museum; Fort Southwick has been sold to the Fort Southwick Company who have interesting plans for its future; Fort Widley is owned by Portsmouth City Council; and Fort Purbrook has been leased by the council to the Portsmouth Youth Activities Committee.

The defensive rôle of Portsdown also came to prominence during the Second World War when the huge shelters were dug into the chalk to house Portsmouth residents during the dark days of the blitz. The London Road shelter had its entrance in what is now the Cliffdale Gardens caravan park, and the Wymering shelter was entered from the Wymering chalk pit. Many Portmuthians spent long nights under the chalk as the bombs rained down on the city.

One of the most distinctive buildings on the ridge must surely be the art deco construction that has always dominated the skyline and would probably have been known to most Portmuthians as ASWE or to explain the acronym, the Admiralty Surface Weapons Establishment.

The 46-acre site – officially known as Portsdown Main – was designed in the 1930s, but the war intervened and the plan did not resurface until about 1947, when it was decided that an Admiralty Signals Establishment (ASE) should be built on War Department land on Portsdown, siting it near Fort Southwick, riding on the fort's important role in the war. Eventually the complex became the Admiralty Research Establishment (ASE), then ASWE, followed by Defence Evaluation and Research Agency (DERA) and finally the Defence Research Agency (DRA).

The clearance and levelling of the hilltop and the building of the first of the eventual 32 buildings began in 1950. Much of the chalk that was removed was passed on to local farmers who used it to harden their drives and pathways.

Just to the west of Fort Southwick are the huge football-pitch sized underground storage tanks holding fuel oil, the pipeline from which still runs down through Portchester to Foxbury Point at Gosport, although it is now redundant and has been filled in. Because of the proximity of such a fuel supply it was decided to heat Portsdown Main with oil, and four boilers, originally destined for a destroyer being built at the Clyde were brought by sea to Portsmouth. Each boiler was then taken by road to Portsdown, the first delivery causing early-morning traffic chaos when it was discovered that the huge steel structure was touching the trolley bus power cables in Twyford Avenue, which had to be switched off.

Portsdown Main finally closed its gates on 1 January 1997, was put up for sale, and is still on the market. Another Ministry of Defence establishment and the independent science and technology company QinetiQ use other parts of the site.

But all was not defence on Portsdown. Enjoyment had its time, especially for the days that the fair took over. Originally the fair, which lasted for week in August, was held high on the summit between The George and Widley windmill. The fair attracted riff-raff from all parts of the country, who caused such a problem that a prison was erected at the corner of Widley Lane in which troublemakers were detained until the fair was over. The jail was called the Round-house Prison, and is shown on the 1846 Ordnance Survey map.

When Fort Widley was built the mill was demolished – although Mill Farm still stands near the ruins of Widley Church – and the fair was forced to move on to the lower slopes, where it continued to entertain until the '50s, usually at the Easter bank holidays.

Just north-west of The George stood Portsdown Lodge, a Georgian house which in the early 1900s became the home of Boundary Oak School. The house had previously been in the possession of Jane Austen's brother, Sir Francis Austen, who was Commissioner of Powder for Portsmouth. Eventually the 9-acre site was sold for housing development and, in 1961, the school moved to its present site at Roche Court, near Fareham, but memories of the educational establishment are retained in some of the road names at Portsdown.

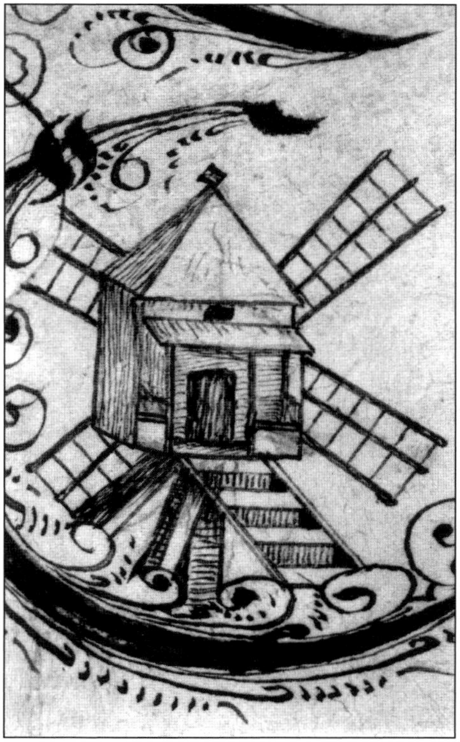

A detail from the original deed of Widley windmill dated 1728.

The crossroads at The George would have been an important stopping point for travellers over the centuries, but the slope was steep and tiring for horses and by the early 1800s a plan was put forward for a tunnel. This forward-thinking scheme never materialised, however tons of chalk were removed to make a deeper cutting and so lessen the incline. A number of human bones were unearthed during the excavations indicating a Roman burial. The new road was opened on 18 November, 1824.

Charles Harper in his book *The Portsmouth Road* wrote of the crossroads: 'At this point the traveller in coaching times came within sight of his destination. Painfully the old stagers climbed up the steep ascent of Portsdown Hill before the road was lowered by cutting through the chalk at the summit, about 1820, and grumblingly the passengers obeyed the coachman and walked up the hill to save the horses. But when they did reach the crest of the hill such a panorama met their gaze as nowhere else could be seen in England: Portsmouth, the harbour, Gosport, the Isle of Wight, and the coastline for miles on either hand lay spread out before their eyes as daintily as in a plan, and smiling like a land of promise.'

Today from the summit of the hill a Portsmouth of a more modern age is spread out before the visitor, but it still can fairly be described as an unrivalled panorama.

Anthony Triggs
Portchester, 2005

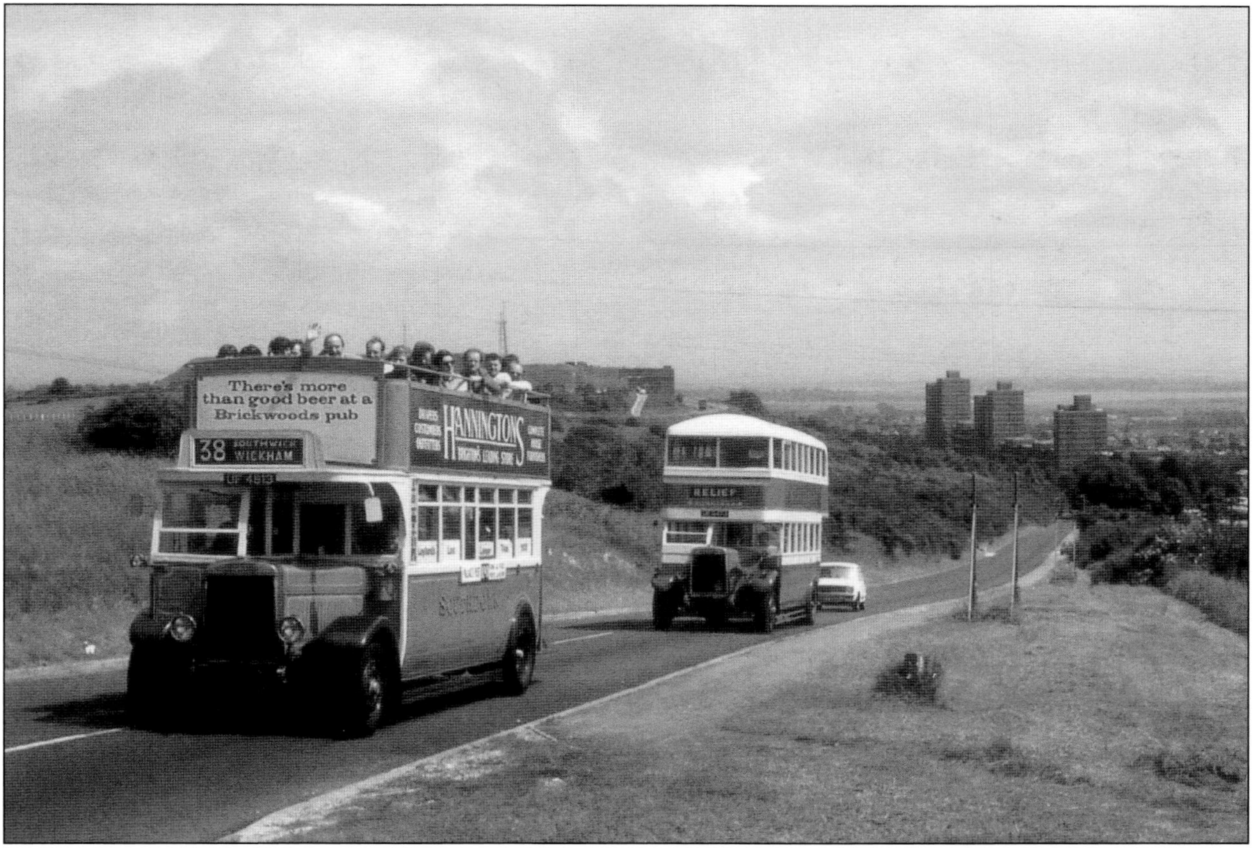

A superb study by Bruce Oliver opens this collection of Portsdown images. On a bright June day in 1981 two vintage double-deckers are taking enthusiasts on a 'special' outing over the hill to the Meon Valley. As they travel on the 1929 and 1930 Leyland Titans, with the ill-fated Portsdown Park in the background, it is interesting to wonder how many of them could have pictured the pastoral look the hill would have had in the past, or imagine the changes the future would bring.

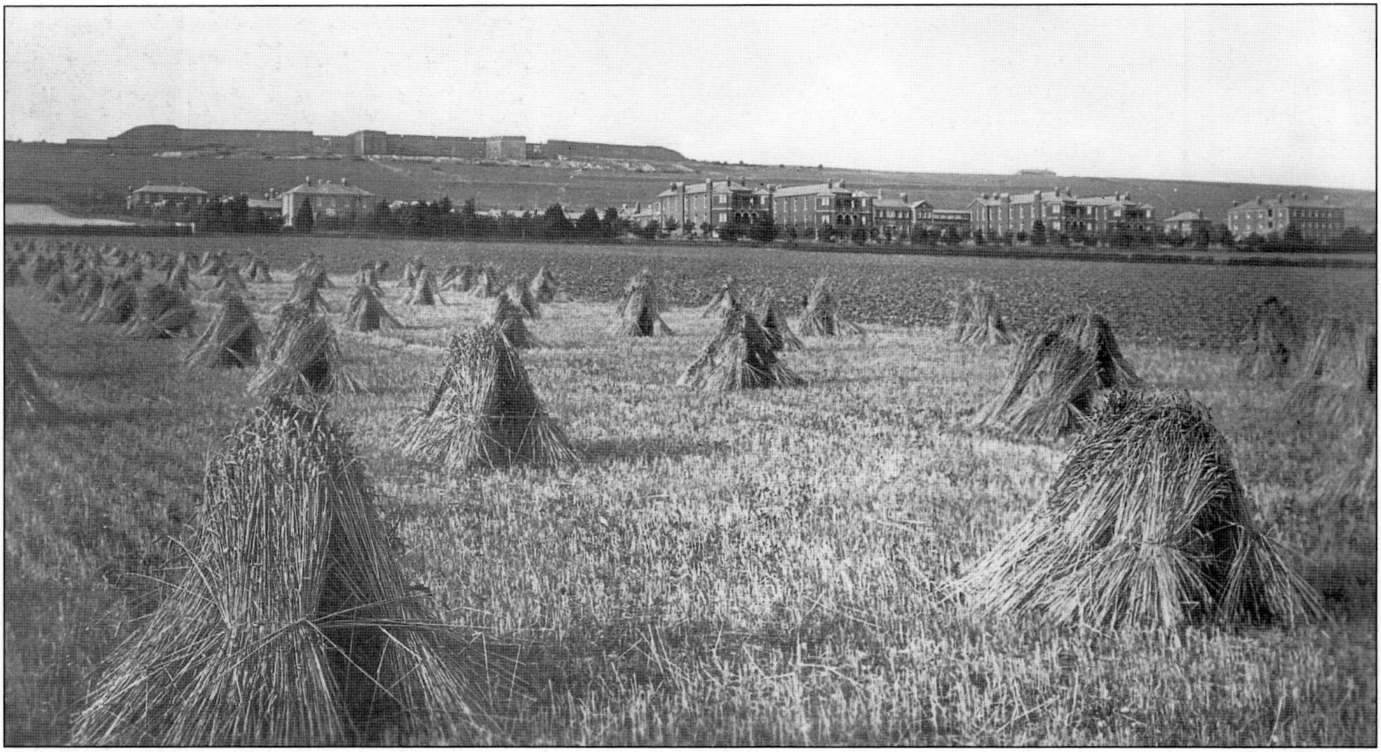

These haystacks make an evocative sight. The social commentator William Cobbett, writing in the late nineteenth century said of Portsdown: 'Eight miles of cornfields, here the first sheaf is cut in England.'

Before the war sheep were a common sight on the higher slopes of Portsdown, with arable farming undertaken lower down. This picture was a popular postcard produced by Southampton photographer F.G.O. Stuart. Francis Godolphin Osborne Stuart was born in Scotland in 1842 and started work as a carpenter and camera maker in Aberdeen. His business developed into that of a photographer in London and in 1883 he moved to Cromwell Road in Southampton. Stuart started to produce commercial postcards in 1901.

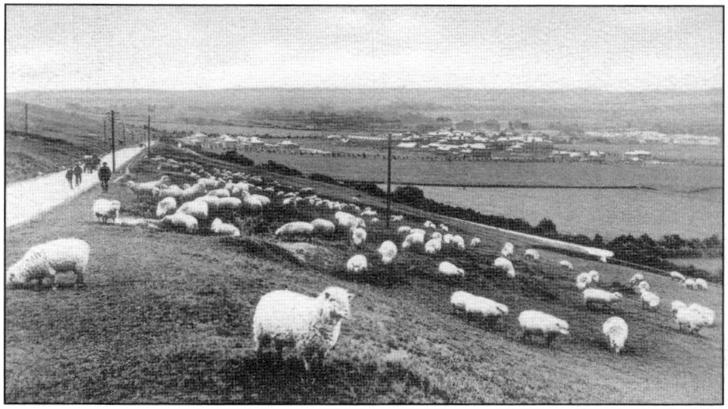

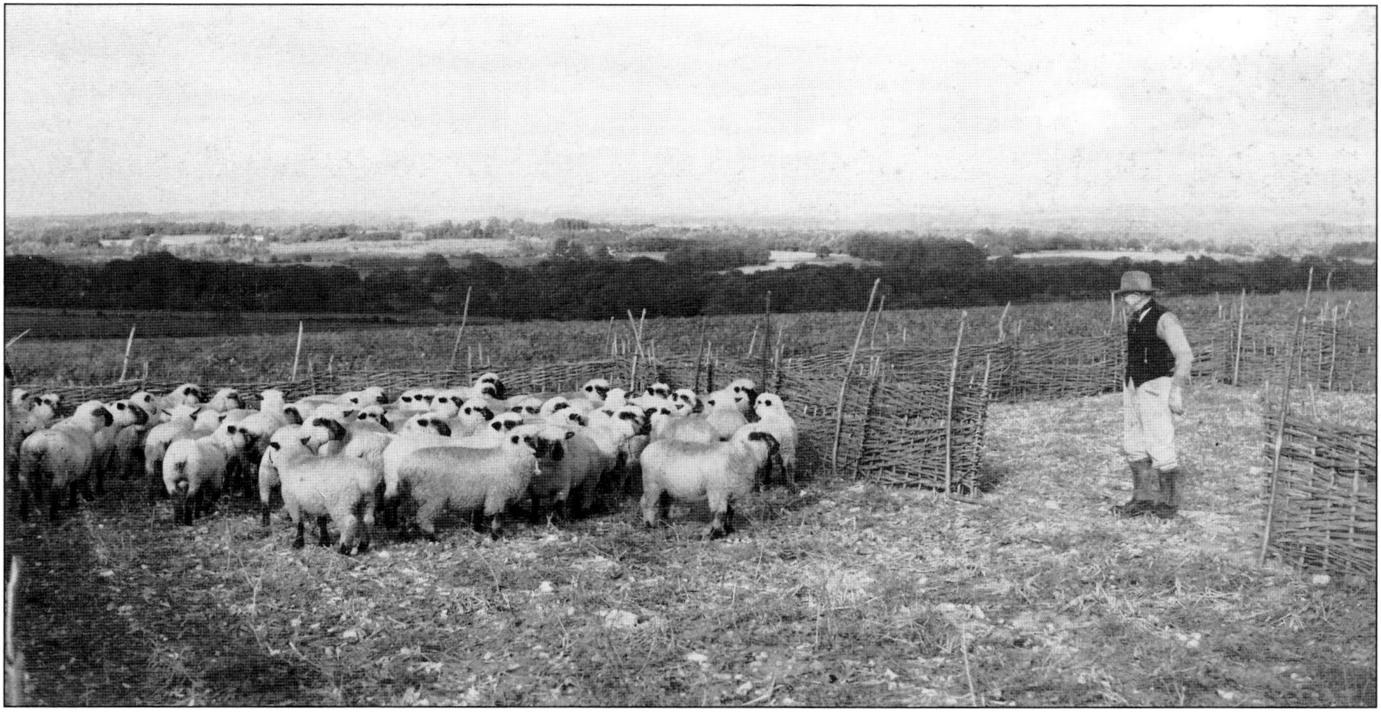

A farmer evokes a rural scene as he tends his flock of sheep on the slopes of the hill near Boarhunt.

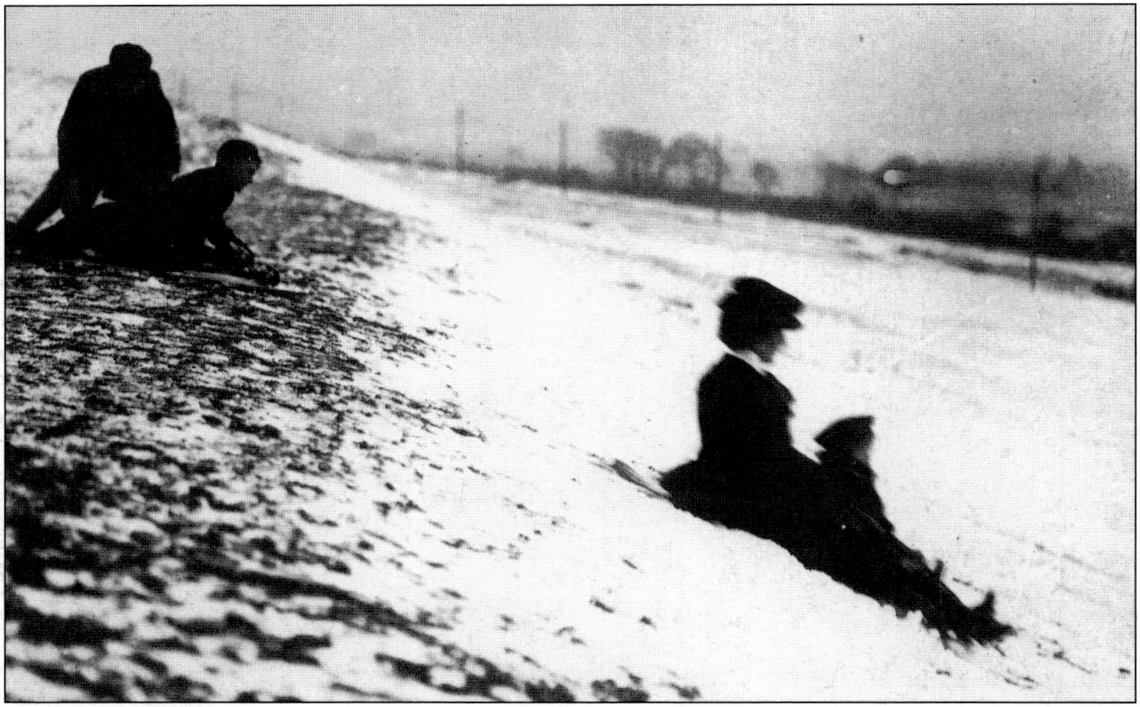

The snow-covered slopes of Portsdown Hill have always provided fun for anyone – of any age or sex – who can lay their hands on a toboggan of sorts, even back in Edwardian times.

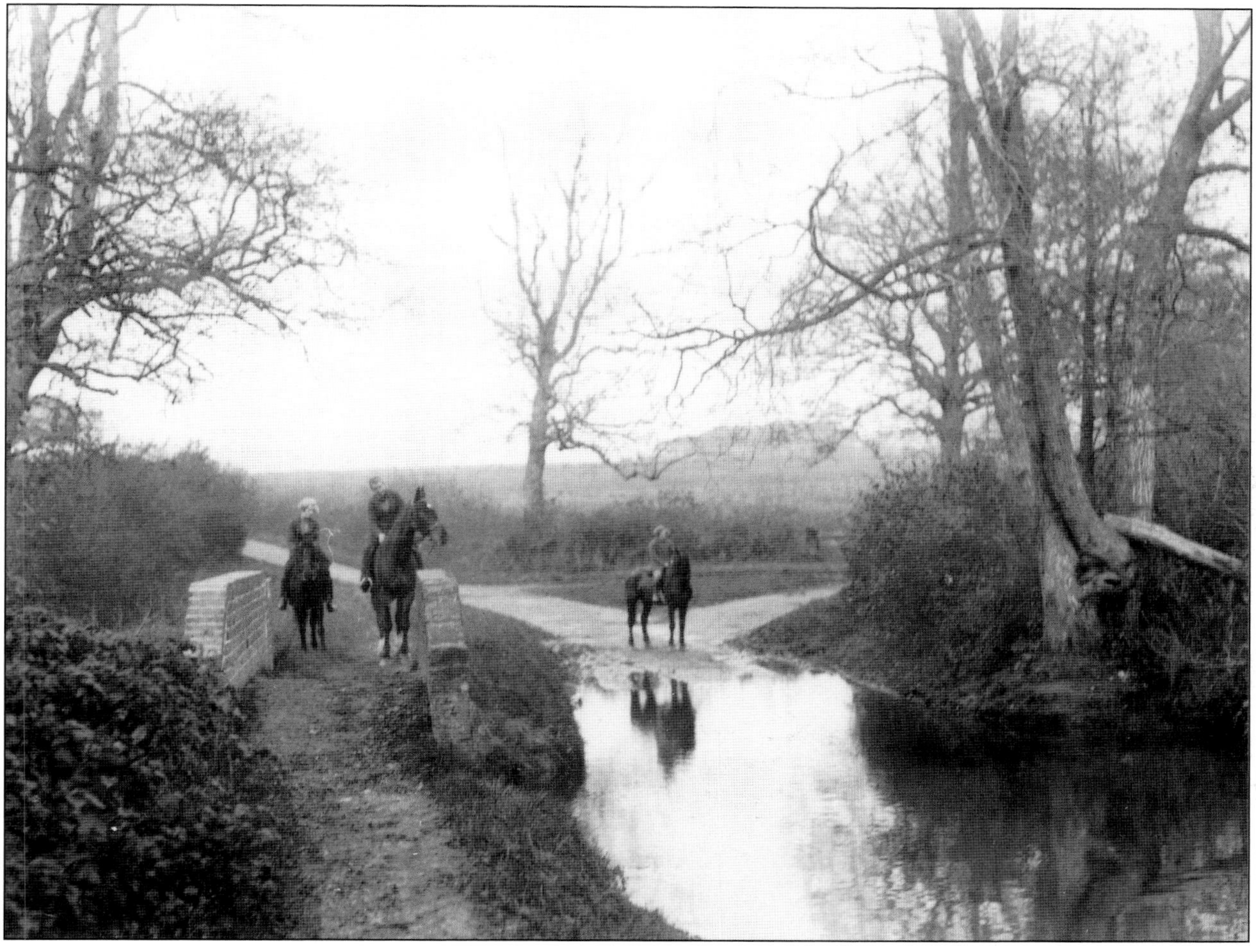

Winter beauty at Pigeon House Lane, where this group of riders takes a camera call in November 1932.

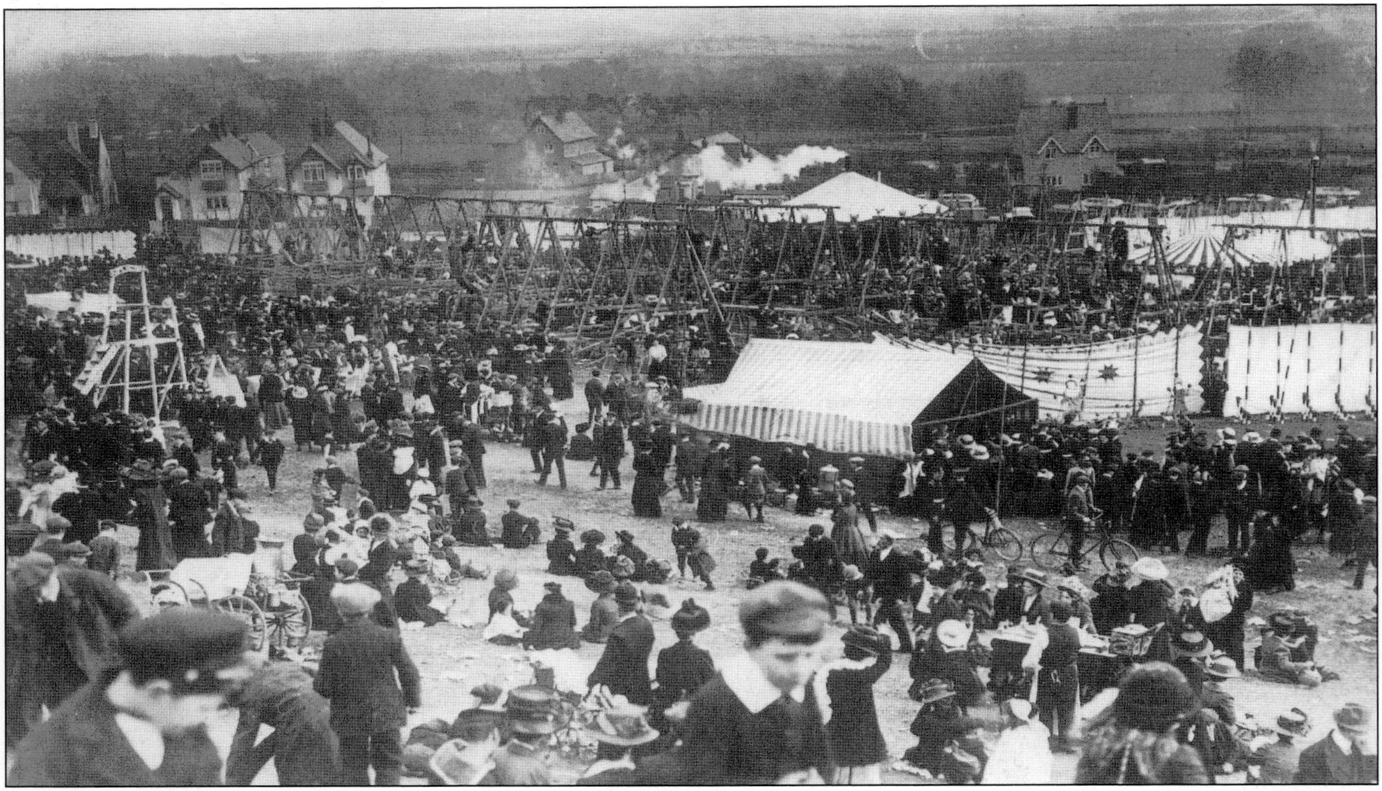

Above and opposite: *Swing boats, roundabouts, ice cream sellers and puffs of steam from the traction engines stand out sharply in this series of pictures depicting the fun of Portsdown fair at the turn of last century.*

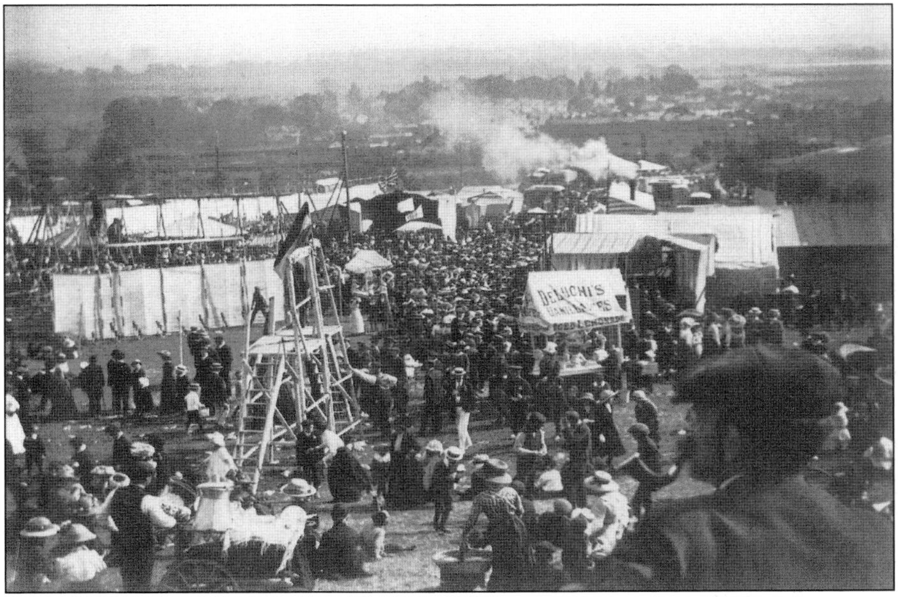

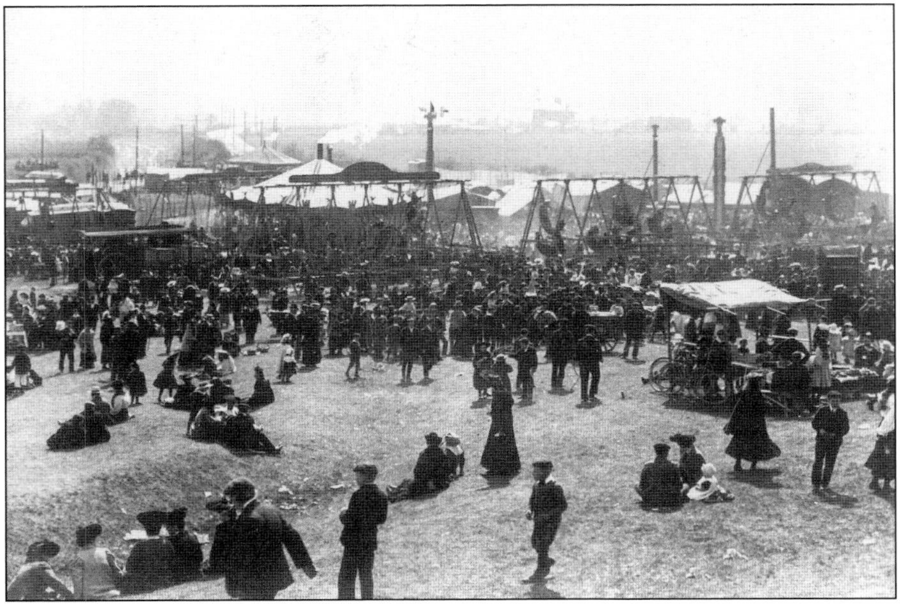

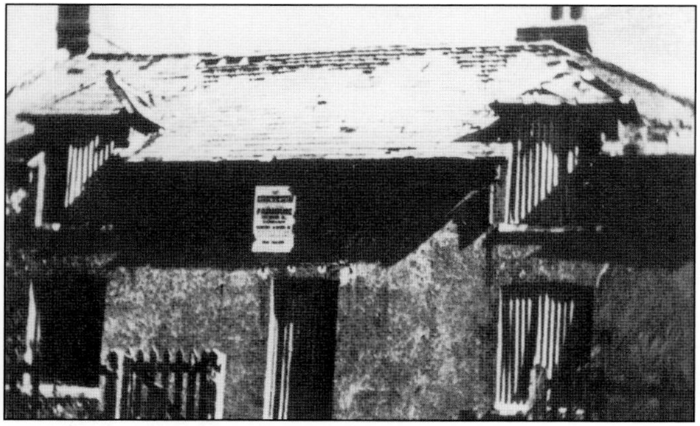

Near the site of the fair there was a small stone-built dwelling called Fairhouse Cottage. It was believed that it was built at the crossroads of the old drovers' track and was given the name later because of its proximity to the fair. In its time it served as a beer house for the construction crews building the forts, and in later years had a bakery added to serve fairgoers. According to Col J.H. Cooke in his book Tales of Ancient Wessex, *it must have been a busy place as there were seven ovens. The cottage was in residential use until the mid 1950s when it was redeveloped into a filling station.*

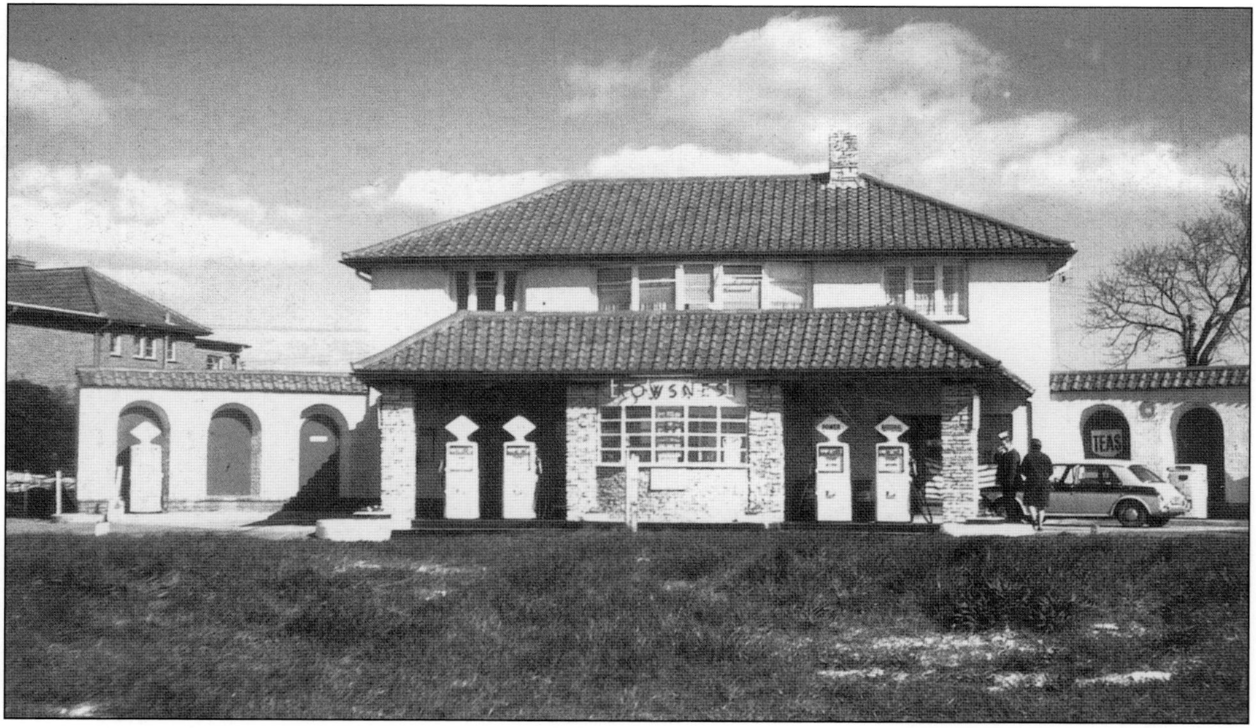

The aptly named Crow's Nest filling station, built on the site of Fairhouse Cottage, is seen here in the mid 1960s. Today the building houses a car sales business.

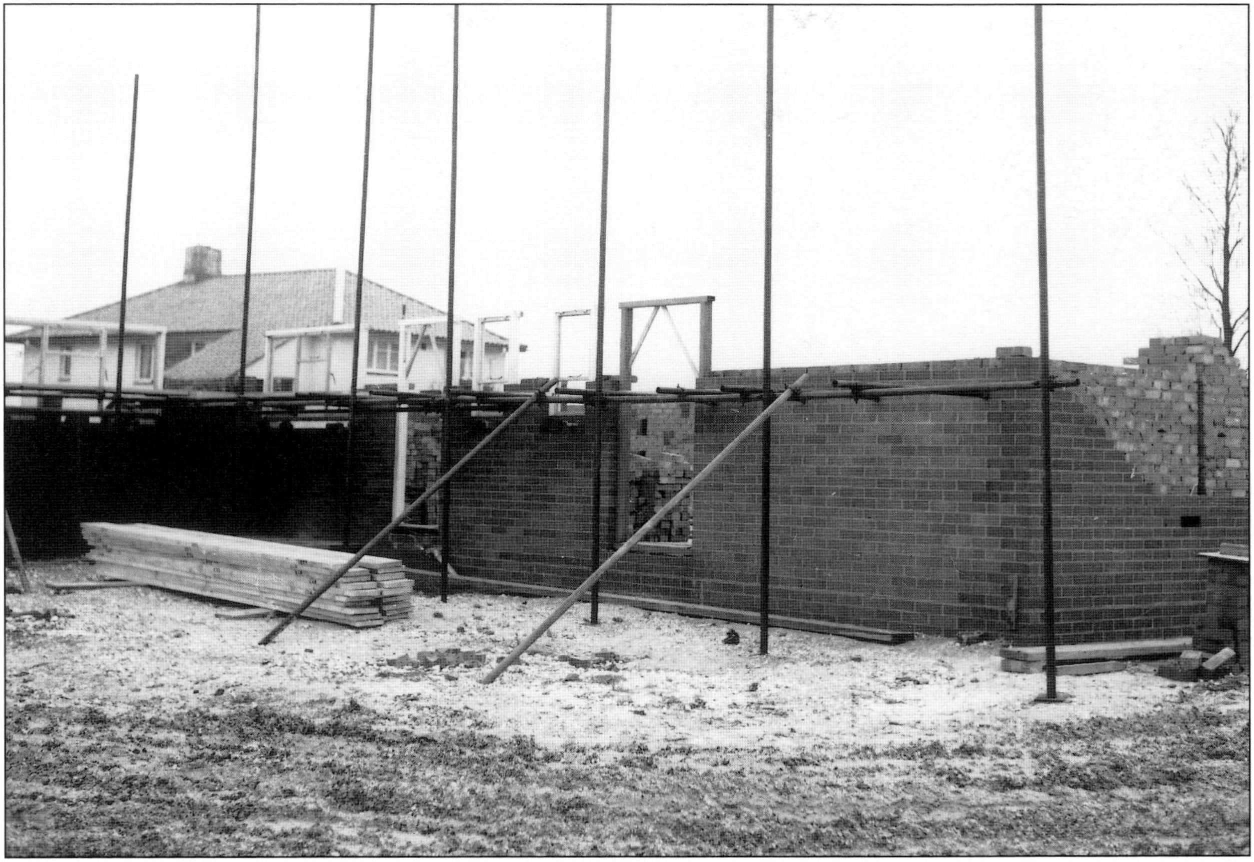

A brand-new public house was built on the summit of Portsdown in the '70s. It was to be called the Churchillian – honouring the famous statesman – and would provide stunning views over the city. This picture shows the construction site in the early stages with the camera facing the rear of the building.

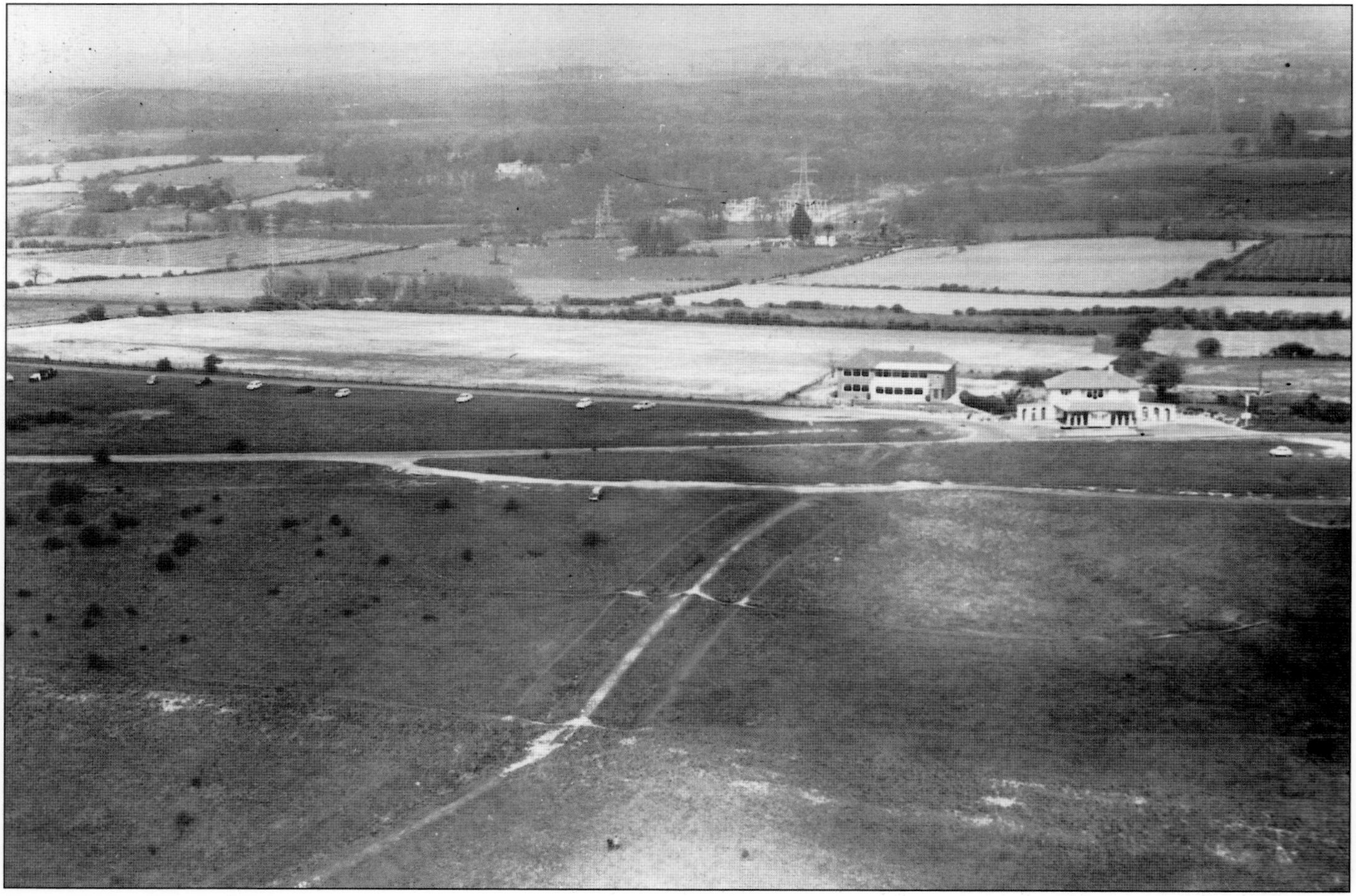

The half-completed pub shows up on the ridgeway in this superb aerial shot by Bob Irwin.

It was not destined to be an easy passage for the pub. The city council declined to grant a licence, and because of this it became known as the Pub With No Beer, after the 1957 popular song by Australian folk singer Slim Dusty. The landlord of the Churchillian used his windows to good effect in his subsequent fight with the council.

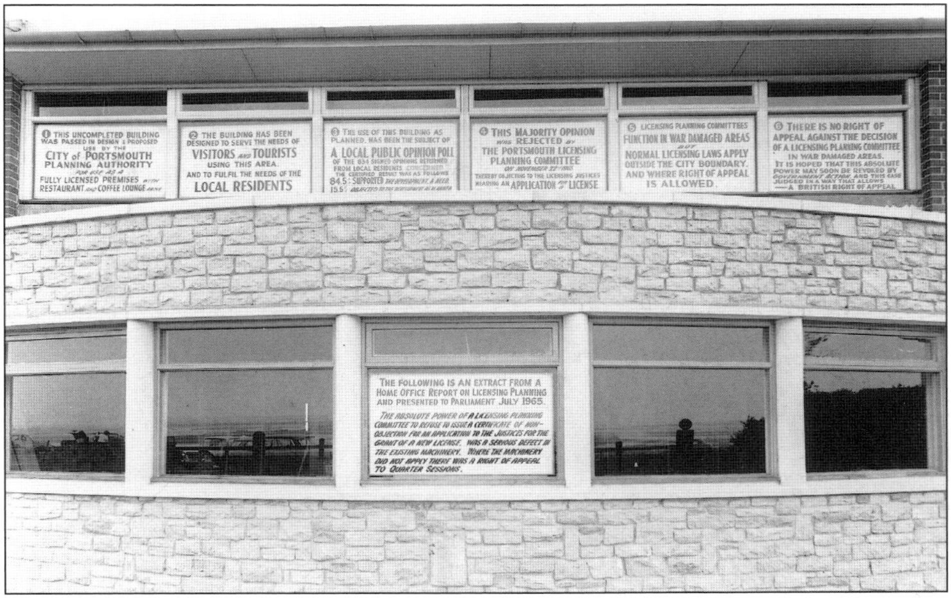

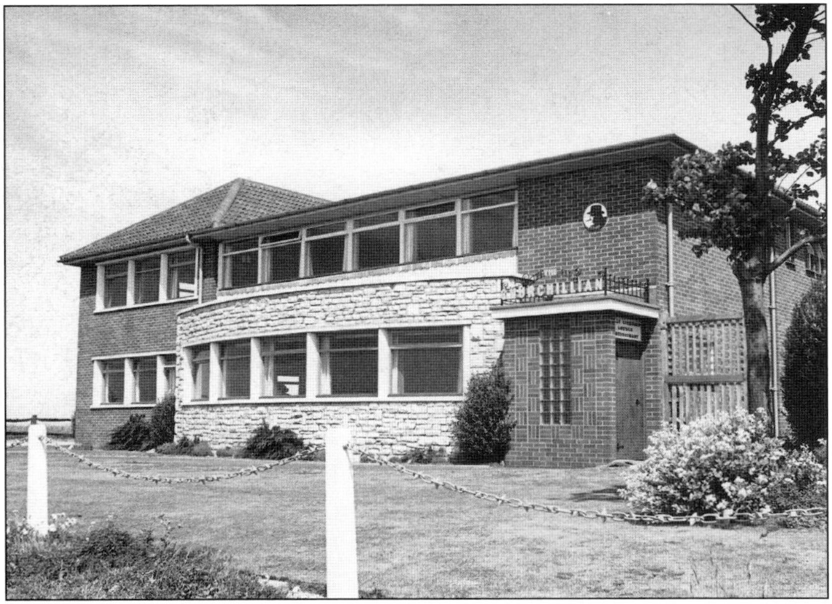

It is now June 1970, the problems are over, and the Churchillian is ready for customers.

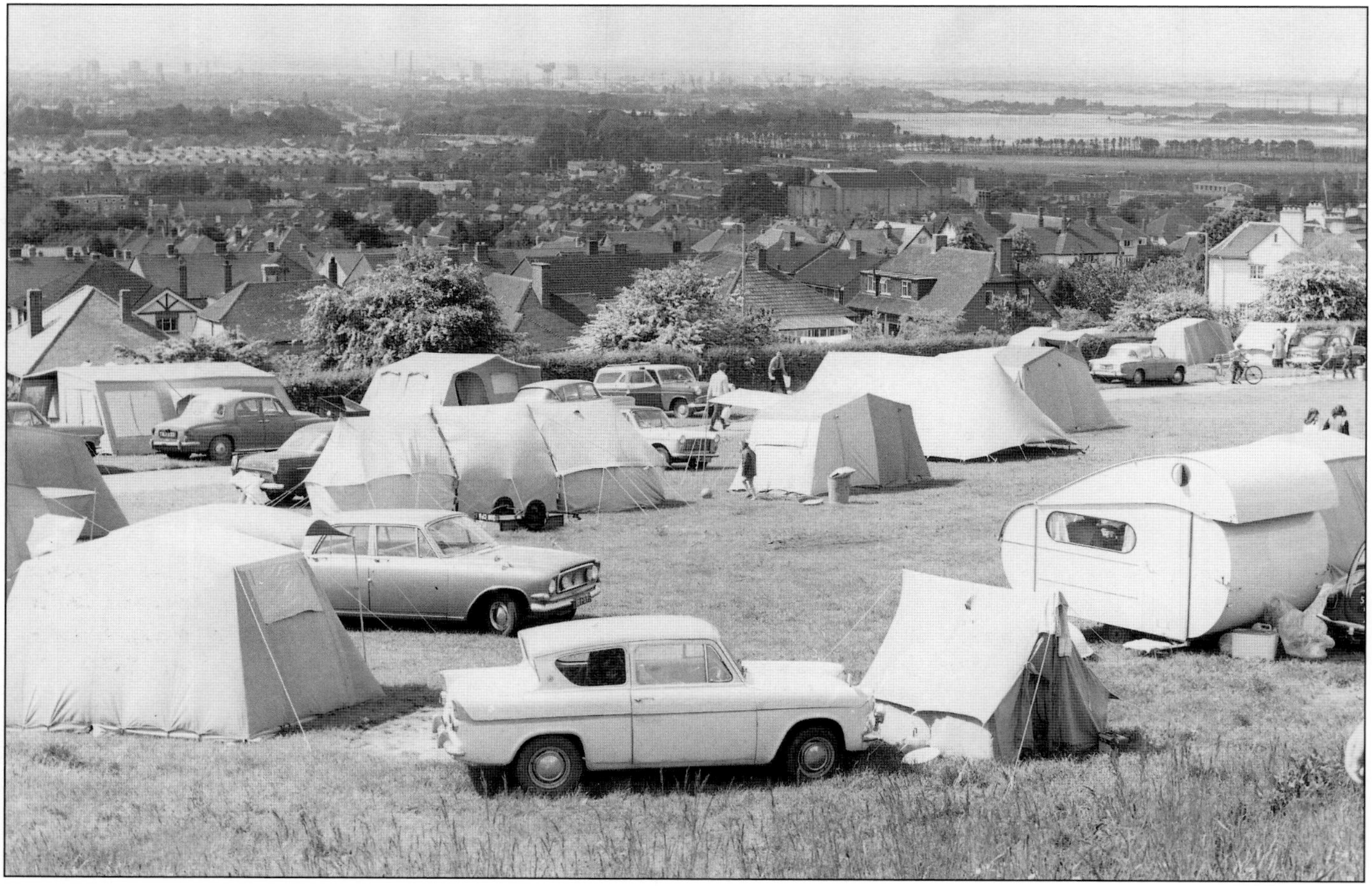

Easter weekend in 1970 brought an influx of campers to the upper hill slopes, happy to take advantage of sunny weather, fresh air, and spectacular views. Tents of all shapes and sizes litter the slopes to the west of the George Inn as the happy holidaymakers settle in for the weekend.

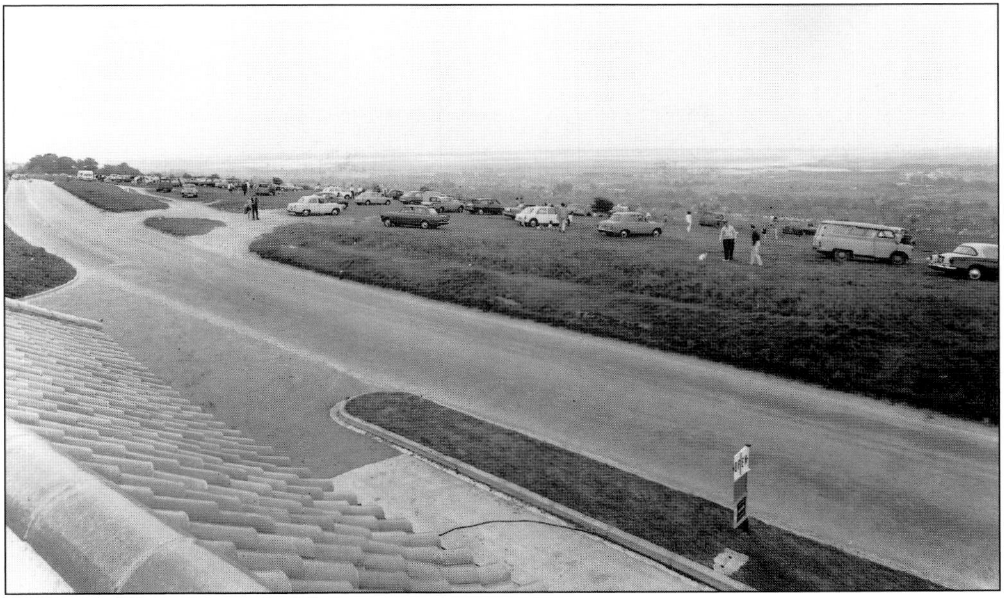

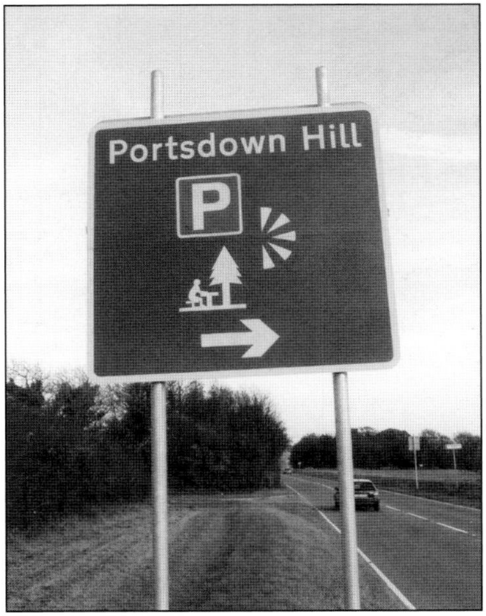

Above: *No tents here, but certainly car owners were happy to enjoy the scenery; however, sometimes an incident with a faulty handbrake and the steep slope caused concern.*

Left: *The council eventually made the area and its counterpart to the east of the George into proper viewpoint areas, and both places are signed for visitors.*

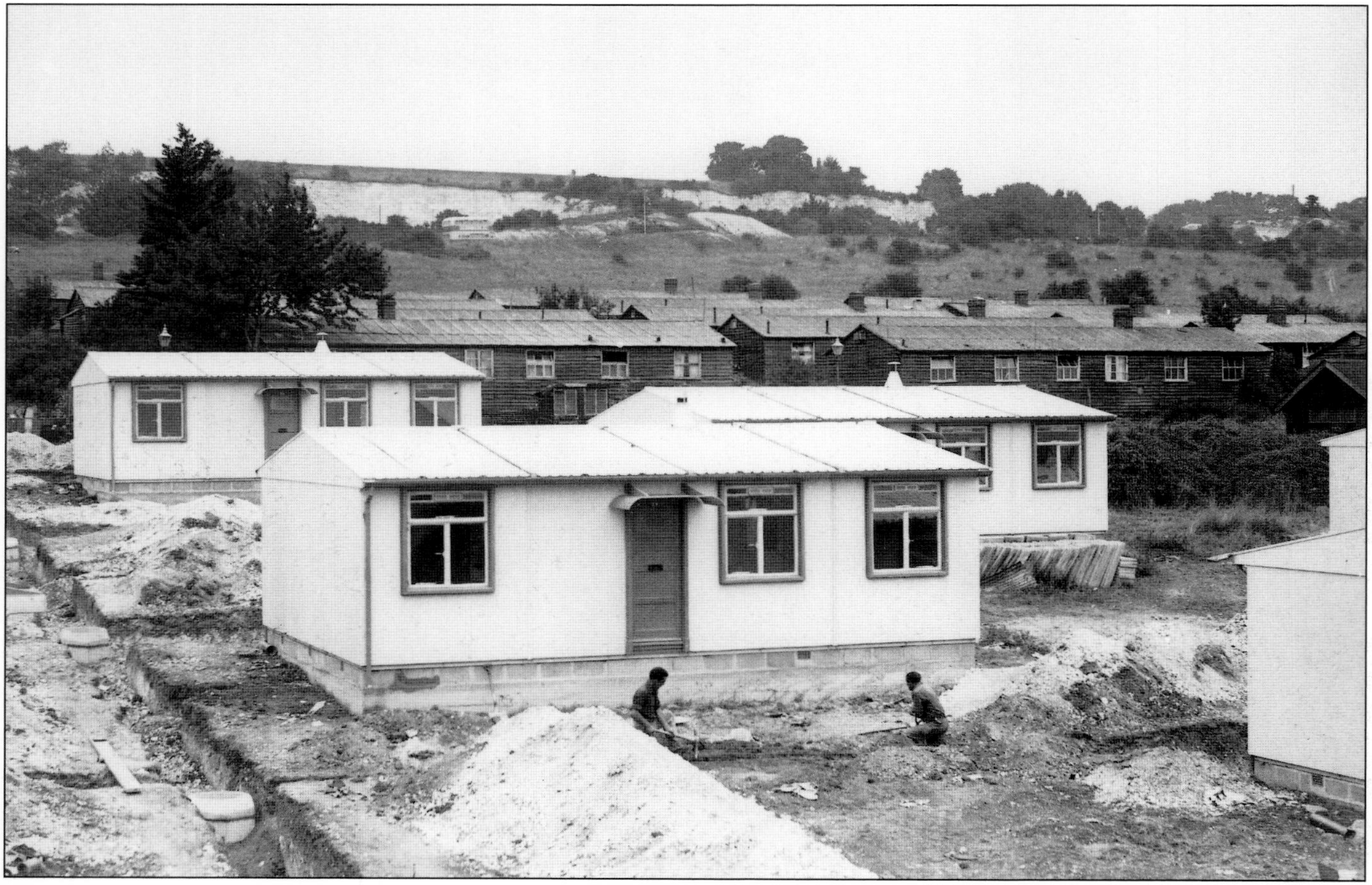

At the end of the war there were thousands of people made homeless by enemy bombing and many soldiers were being demobbed, returning to the UK with little chance of finding a place to live. Prefabricated homes were the answer and all over the country the little grey/white structures were springing up. Portsmouth was no exception with hundreds of prefabs being built along the slopes of Portsdown Hill, the first being opened officially in July 1945. The huts in the background were troop accommodation left over from the Great War.

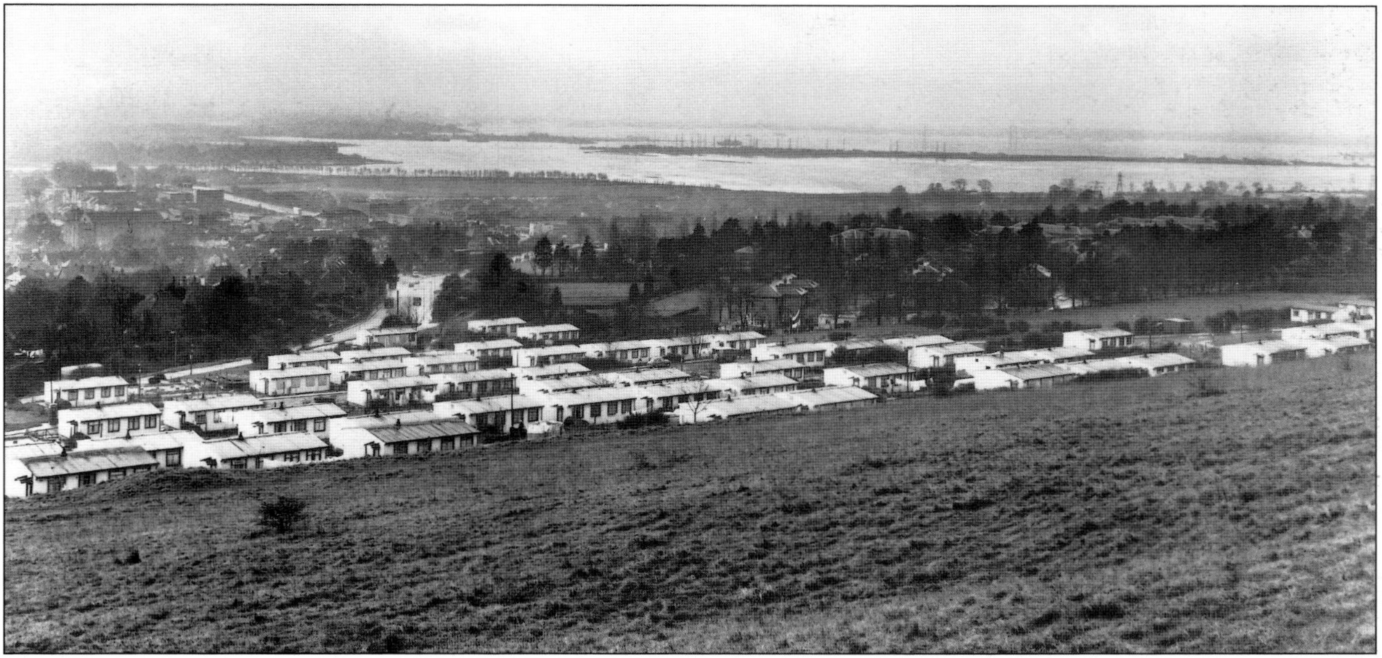

A new town of prefabs is clustered on the hill. With fitted kitchens, built-in appliances and fridges the new homes were far superior to many of those flattened by German bombs.

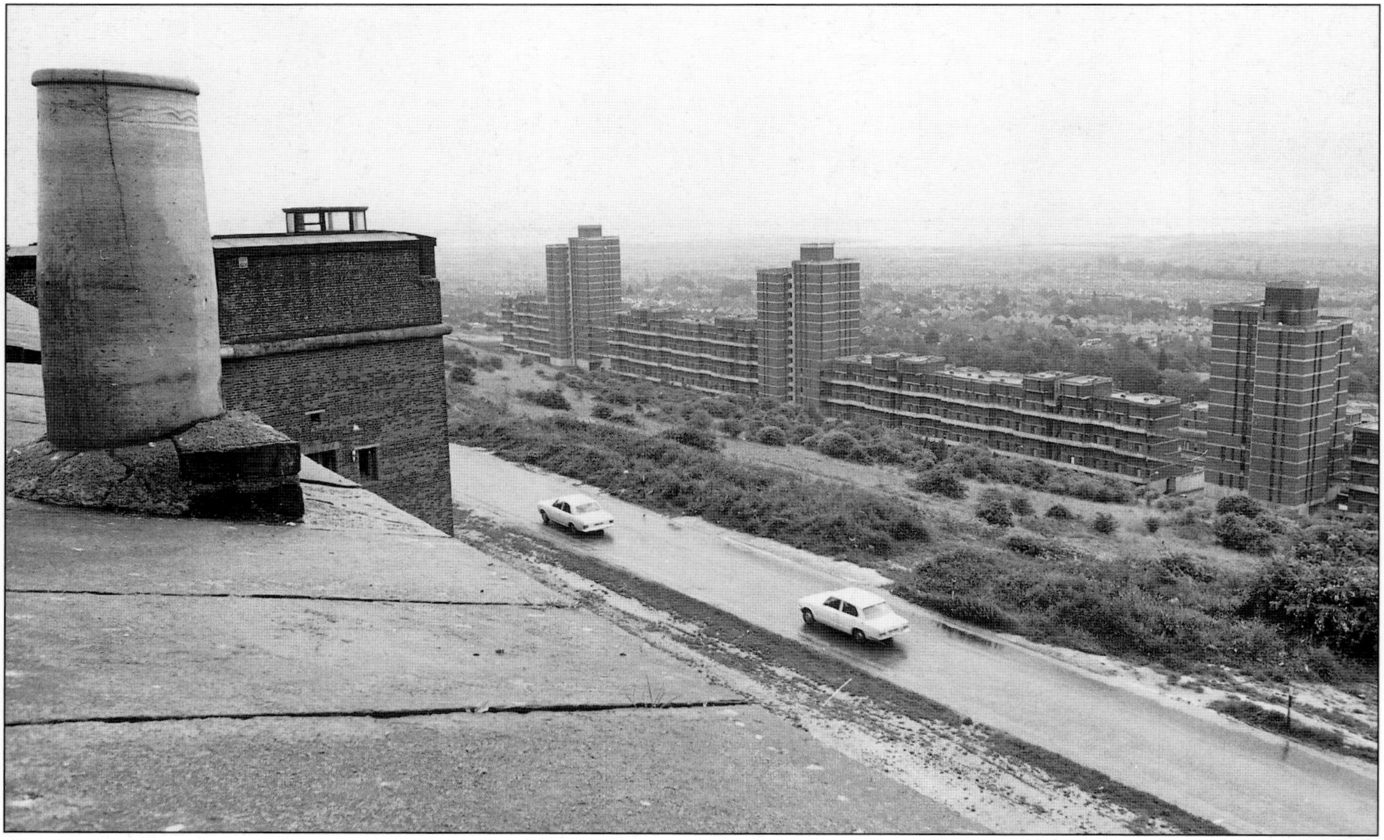

An enterprising cameraman has taken to the top of Fort Widley to gain this unusual view of the ill-fated Portsdown Park housing development, which was to stand for such a short time. In 1965 the city council offered a prize of £1000 for the winning design, and the work started in May 1968. However, the project was beset with problems during the construction period, and more troubles surfaced after the tenants moved in. They complained of condensation and water penetration problems, high rents, poor bus services, and vandalism, and many described the estate as 'the most unpopular place to live in Hampshire.'

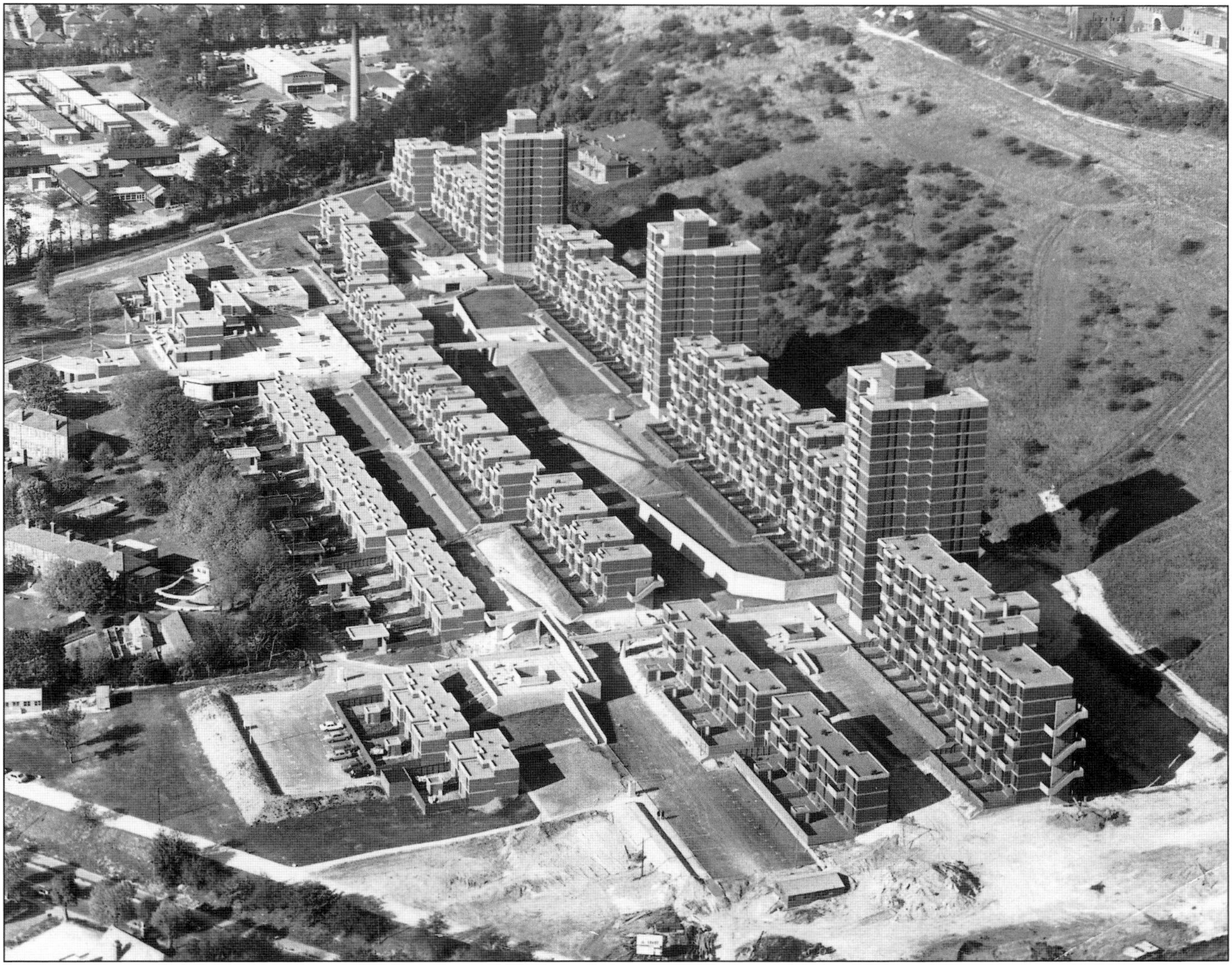

The towers and blocks of Portsdown Park show up clearly in this impressive aerial view. The development was intended to be a showcase for Portsmouth City Council, but instead it became an embarrassment and was demolished after a mere nine years, by which time the council had spent more than £700,000 on technical advice and remedial work

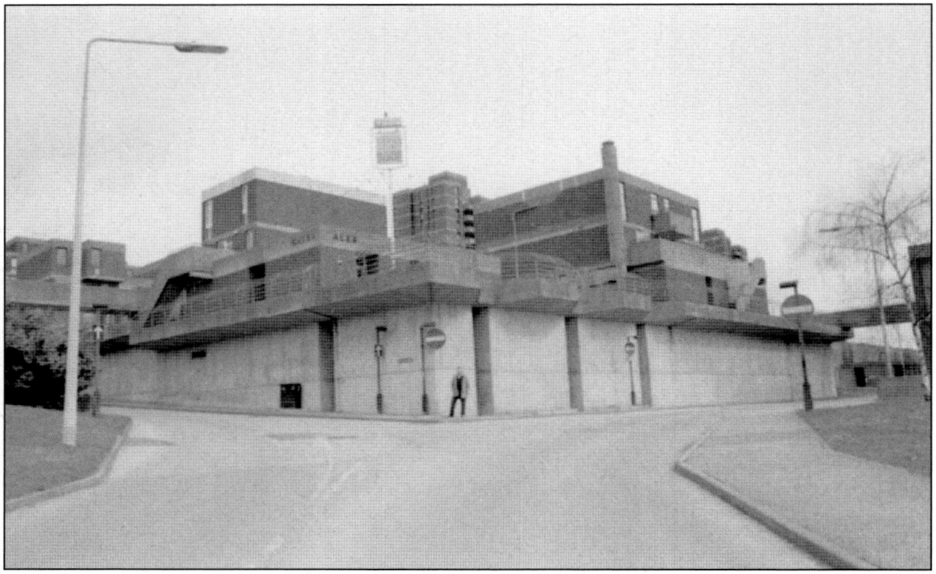

Above: *The Harlequin public house stands empty after all the tenants had been re-housed and the Portsdown Park ghost town was awaiting the demolition crews.*

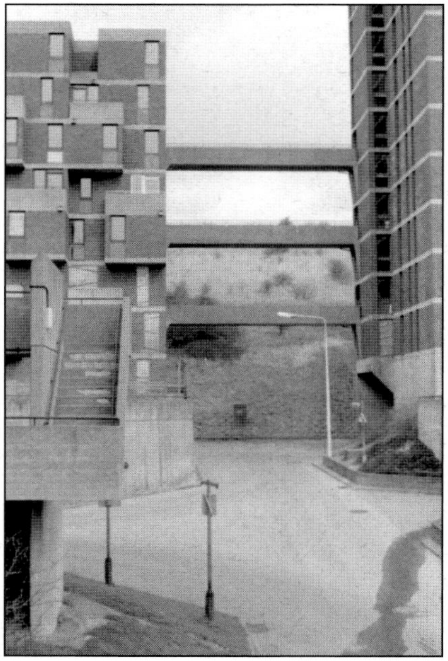

Left: *Empty stairs and walkways bear witness to the sad demise of the Portsdown Park project.*

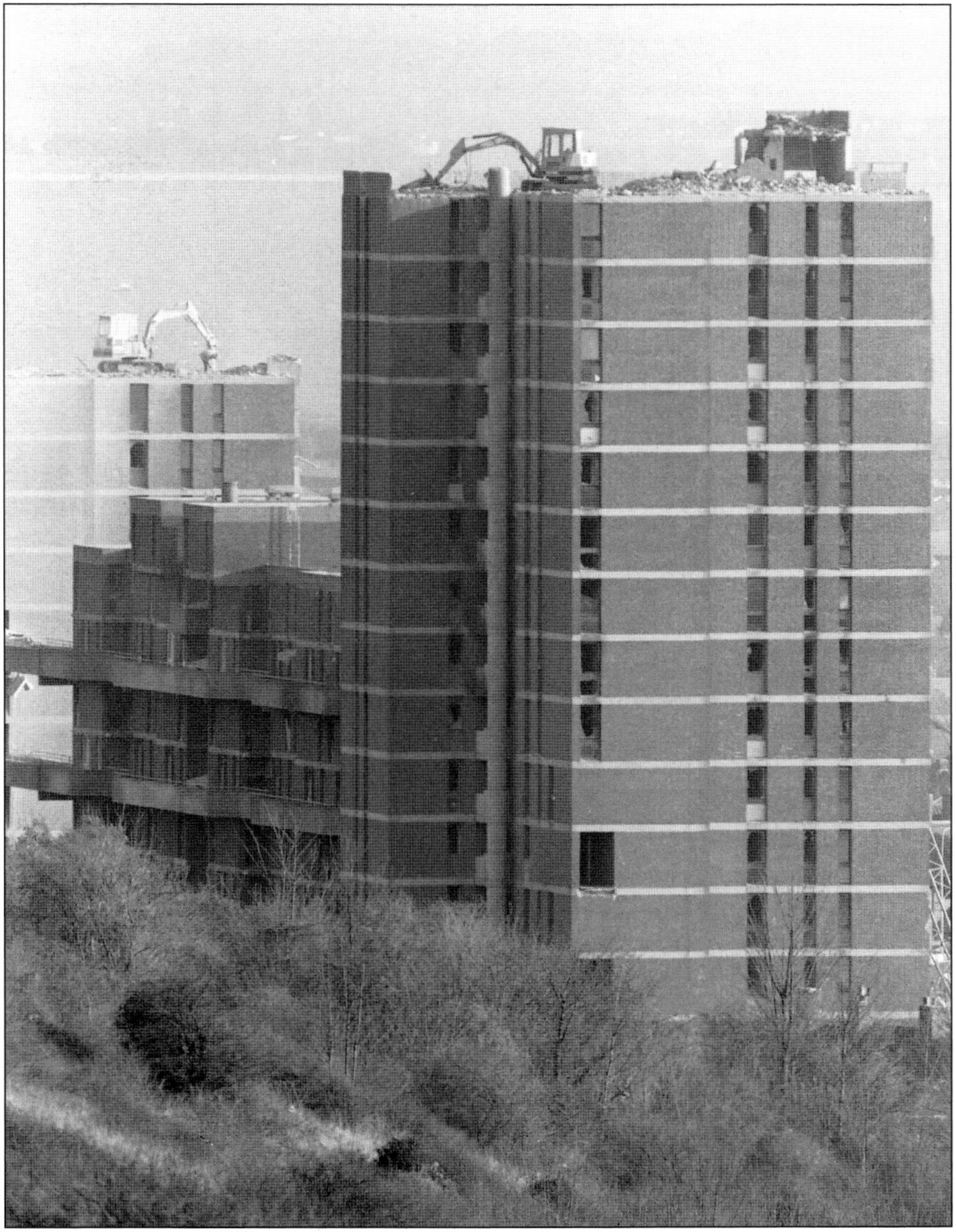

Two bulldozers – lowered on to the roofs of the tower blocks by helicopter – begin the demolition process by working their way down through the floor levels.

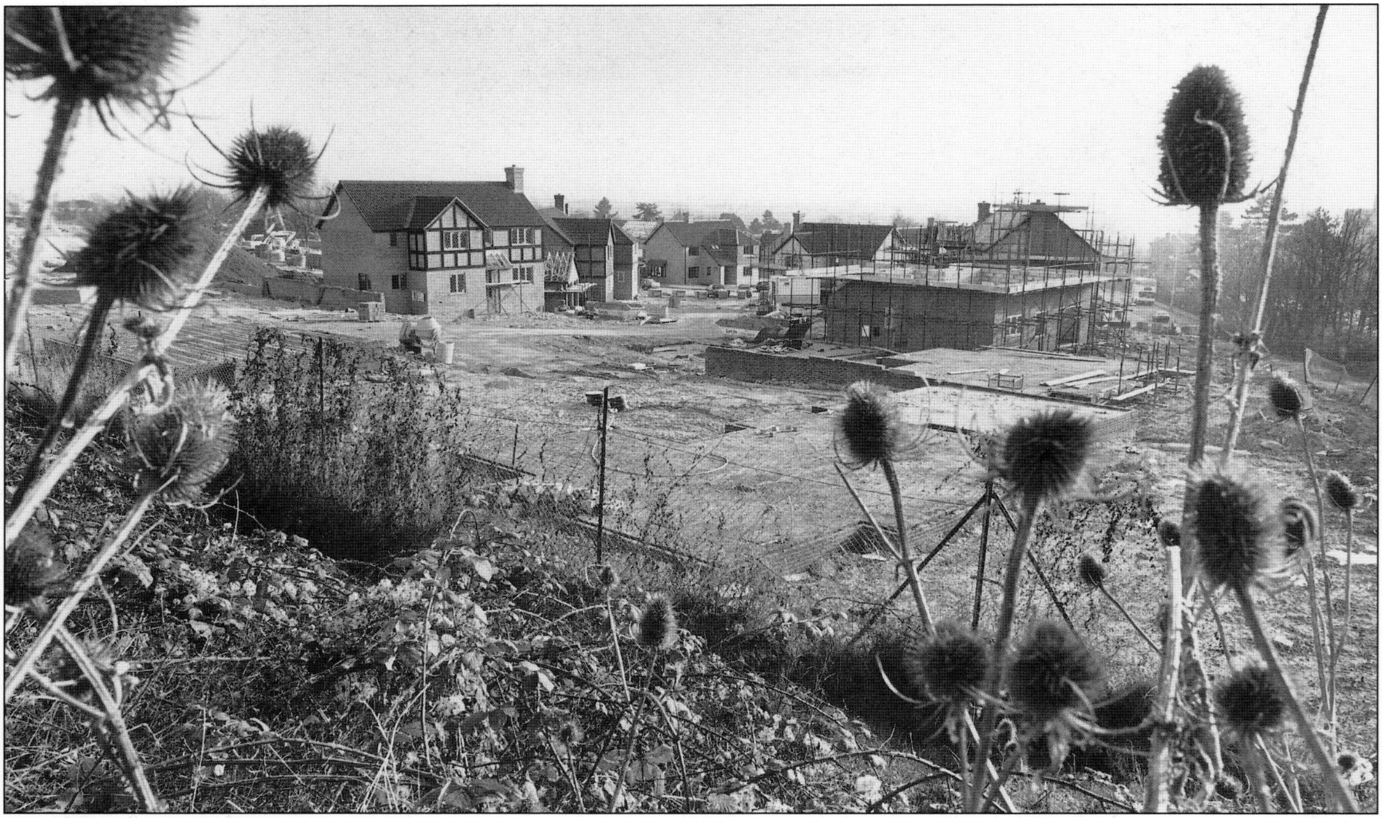

New homes start to take shape on the Portsdown Park site, set to obliterate all traces of the troubled project.

Opposite: *In 1971 the decision was made to dispense with the winding Crookhorn Lane and to provide an easier route for traffic from Portsdown Hill Road. The plan met with some amount of opposition but nevertheless went ahead. The white scar formed as the chalk was cut became known as the Havant Gap. To the left of this stunning aerial view is the eastern edge of Fort Purbrook.*

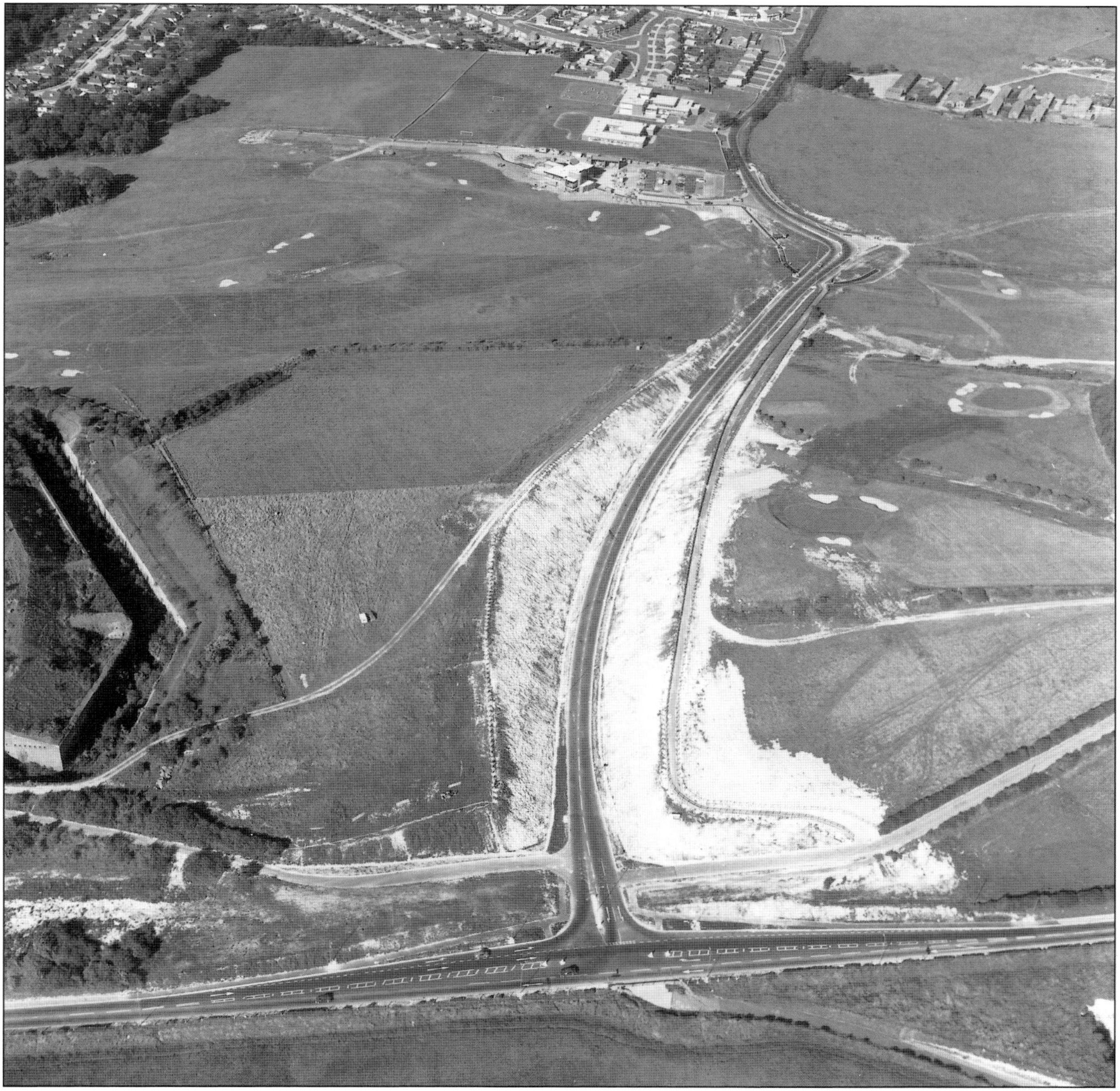

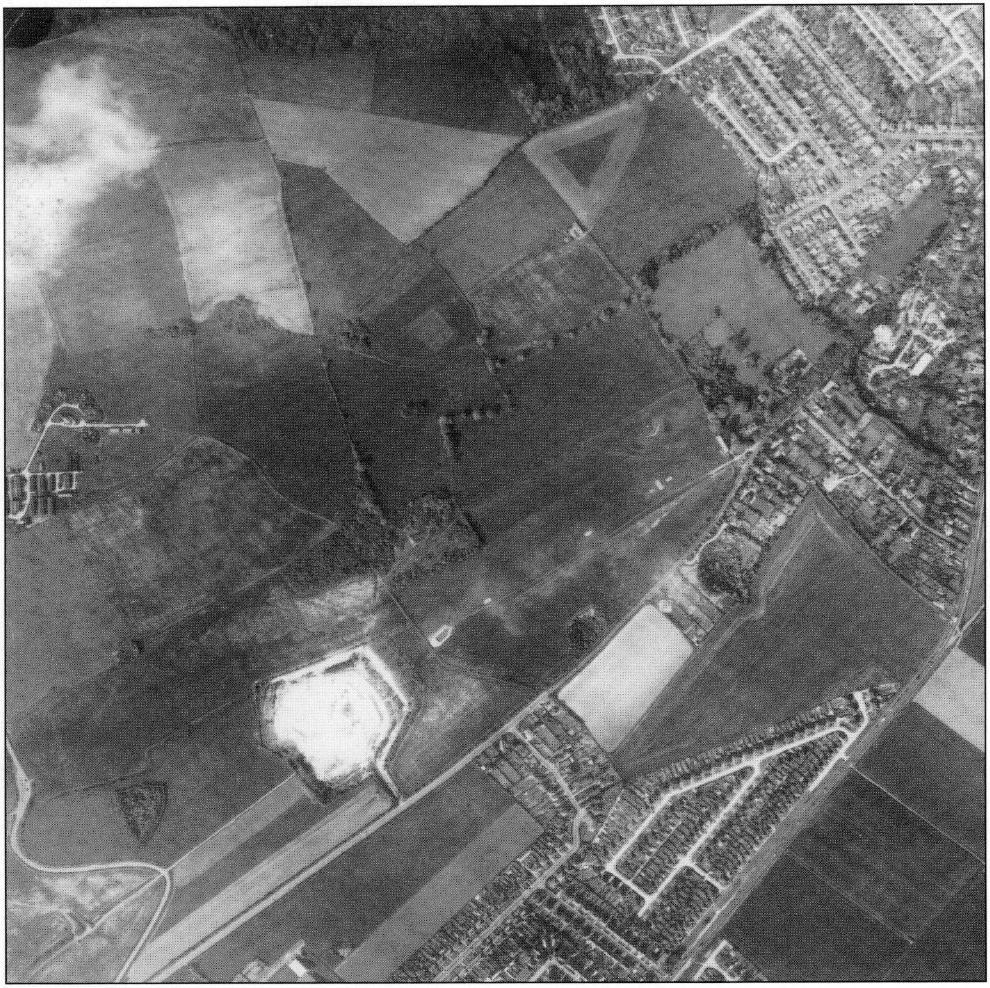

Farlington Redoubt shows up as a white shape on the ridge of Portsdown, while to its left is the shield-shaped area of woodland known as Dead Man's Copse. To the left of the picture can be seen the Morelands anti-aircraft battery site with the group of huts and the AA gun pits still in evidence.

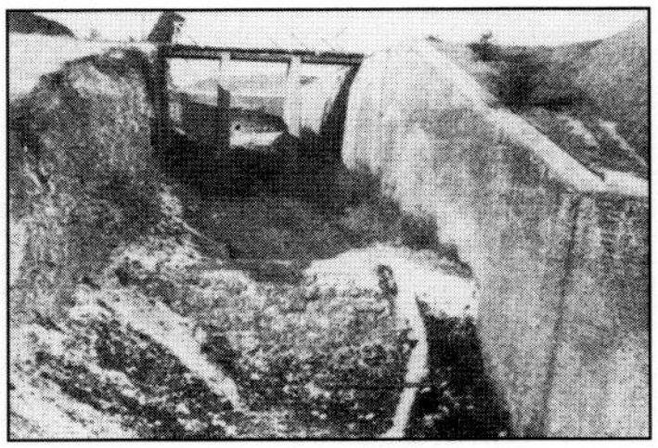

Farlington Redoubt is pictured in the '30s. For a while Havant council had plans to turn the site into a crematorium but the idea was never adopted. The redoubt was eventually demolished in the 1970s and is now a commercial business site.

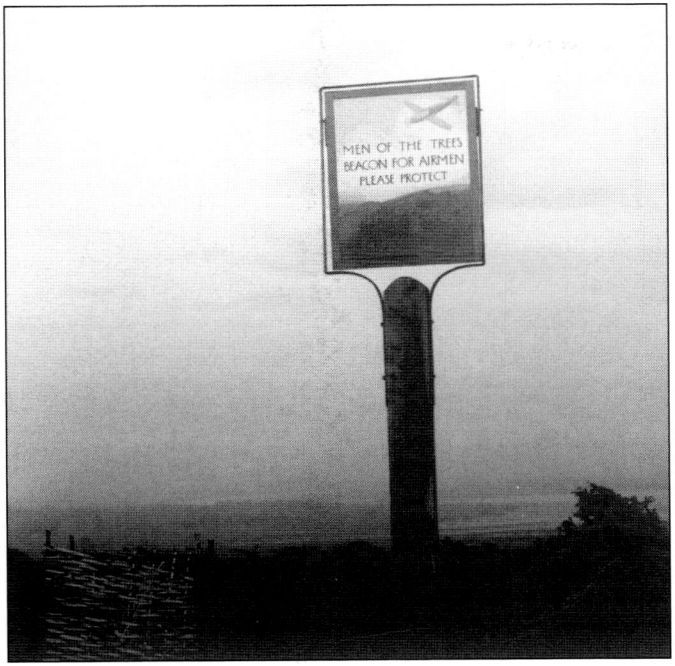

To help our airmen during the dark days of the war the conservation group Men of the Trees erected a navigational beacon on the summit of Portsdown Hill in Dead Man's Copse. After the war, in the 1950s, the group erected small memorial plaques in the copse, of which three remain today. One of the plaques remembers Korean War victims. The site is now on private land. There is also a memorial stone on the downs near the Churchillian public house dedicated to the memory of Sergeant Hubert Adair, whose Hurricane crashed in a nose-dive near Pigeon House Lane. Members of the Wealden Aviation Archaeological Group excavated the aircraft and the remains of the pilot in 1979.

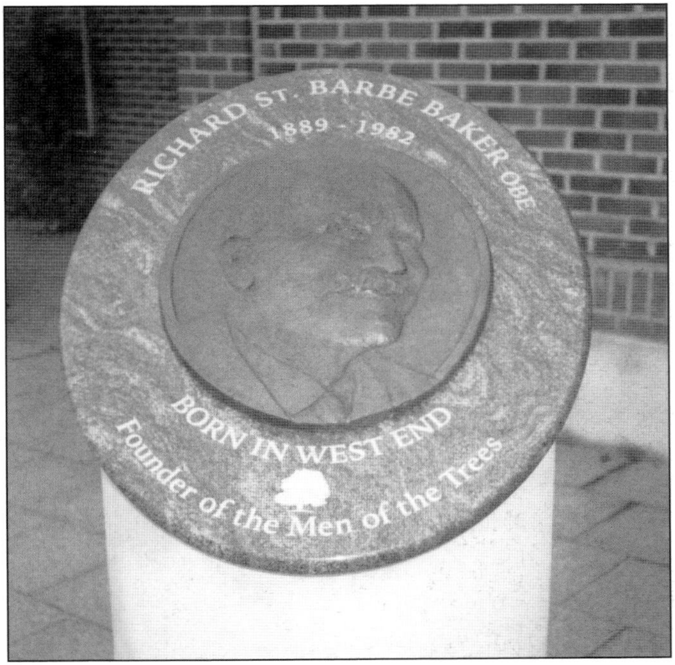

The plinth sited at West End, Southampton, commemorates the birthplace of Richard St Barbe Baker, OBE, founder of the Men of the Trees, who is buried in Canada.

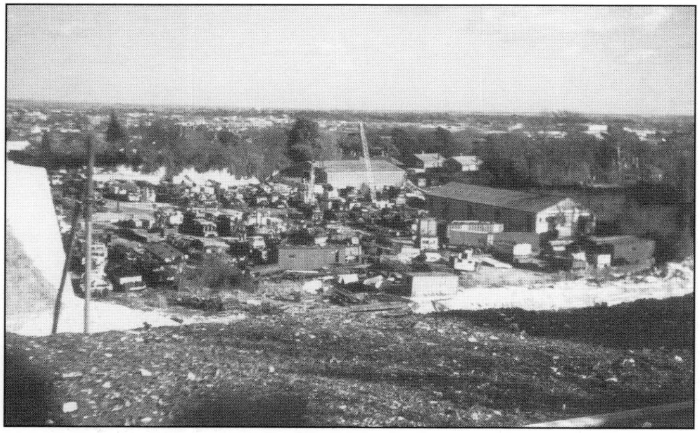

Left: *During the last war the chalk pit at the eastern end of the hill near Bedhampton was used for the storage of munitions. After the war the site was taken over by Southern Counties Demolition (Sullivan's) for the storage of scrap vehicles. This view, showing the huge array of vehicles, was taken by author John Sadden in 1979.*

Below: *Four former Portsmouth Dockyard steam locomotives wait to be scrapped at Sullivan's scrapyard.*

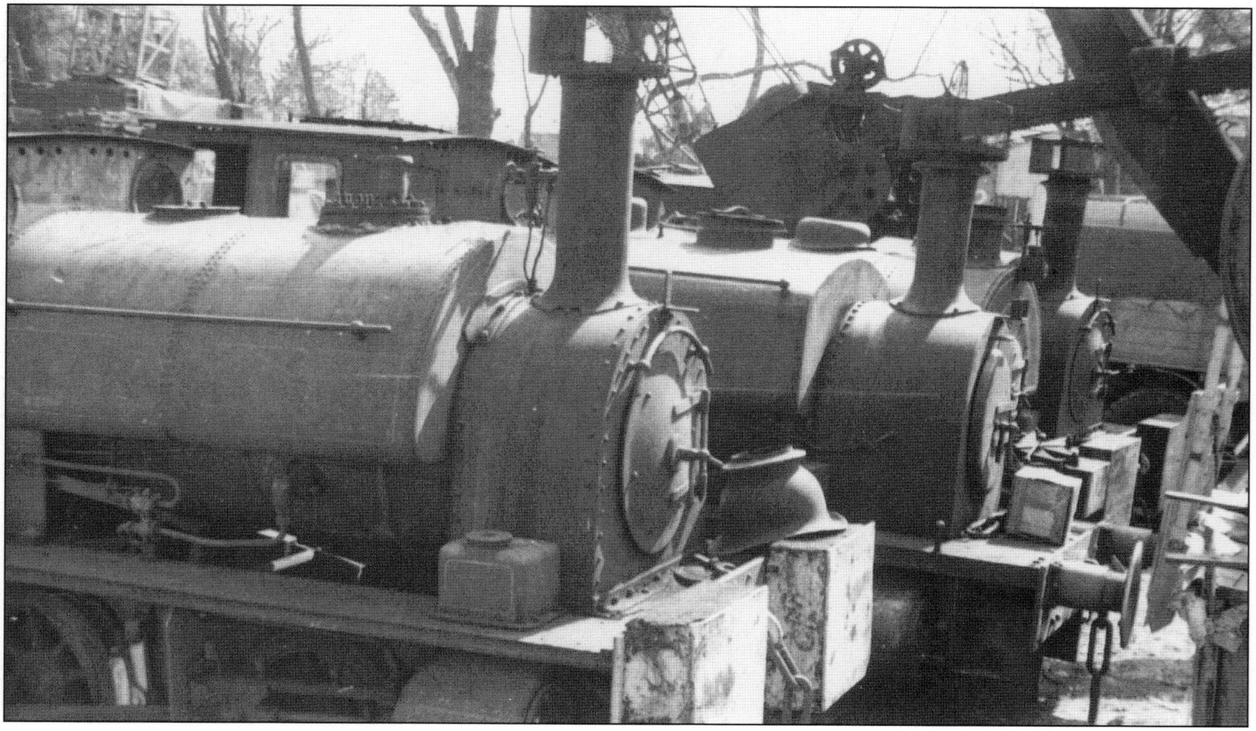

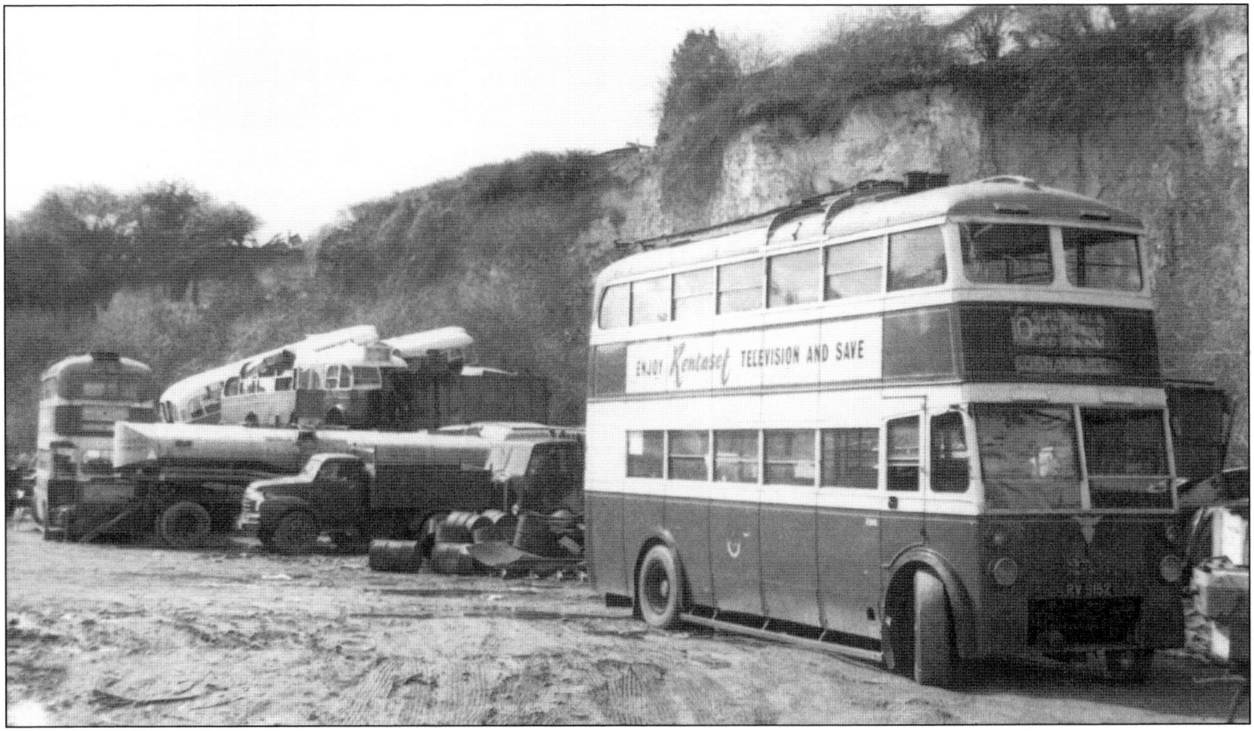

A redundant Portsmouth trolleybus awaits its fate in the yard. This one, RV9152, came into service in 1936 and was originally No 98, but was renumbered in 1938. In the background are some Yorkshire single-deckers whose engines were removed in order for them to be used on local vehicles. Bruce Oliver took these two pictures in April 1961.

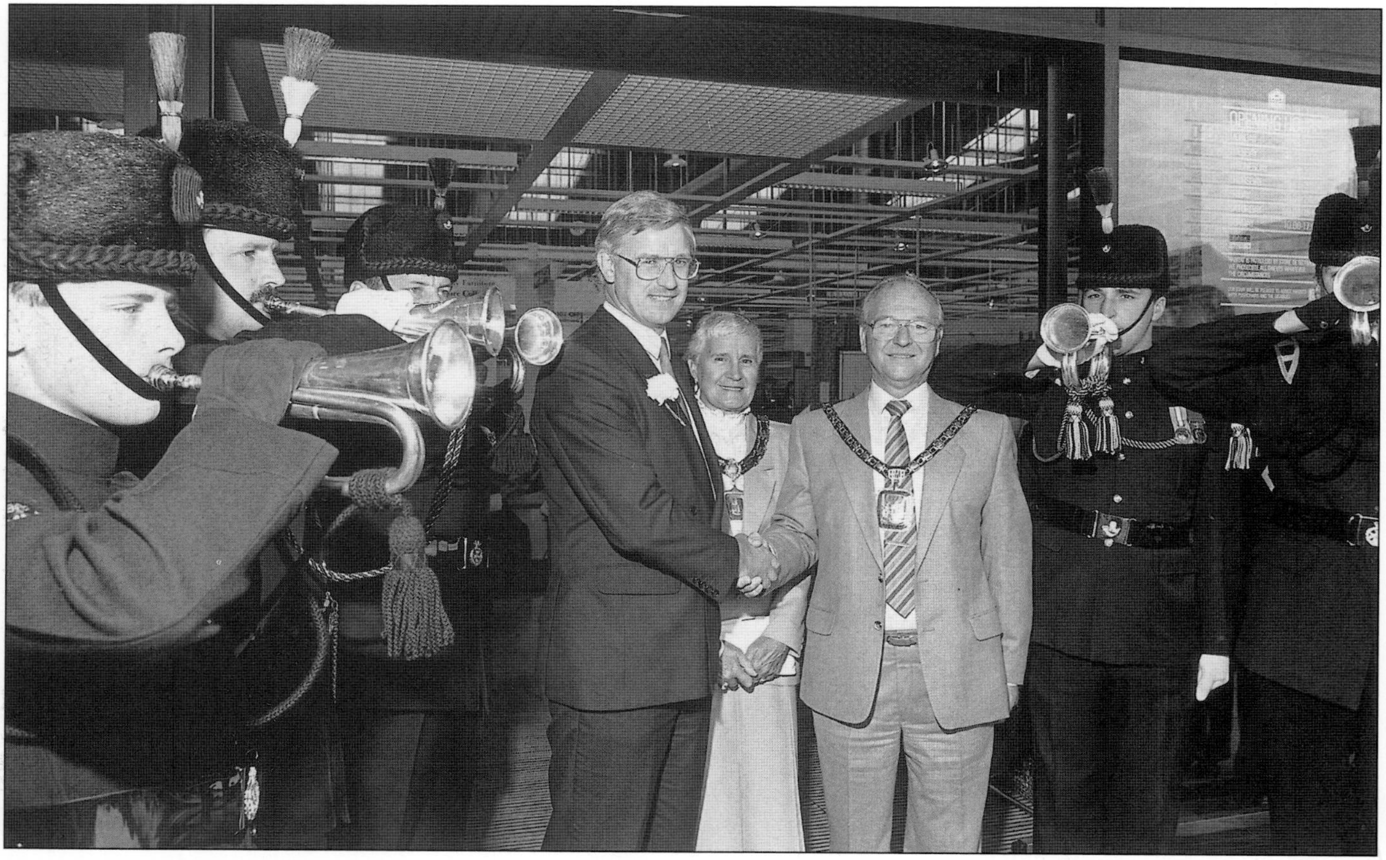

The development of out-of-town shopping led to the chalk pit being cleared. A bowling alley and a new store in the Habitat group was opened – to musical accompaniment by buglers of the Royal Green Jackets – on 22 September, 1988. Store Operations Director Bob Parkes is pictured with the Mayor of Havant, Councillor Peter Osborne, at the opening ceremony. The Habitat store had a short life and the building now is a Homebase DIY store.

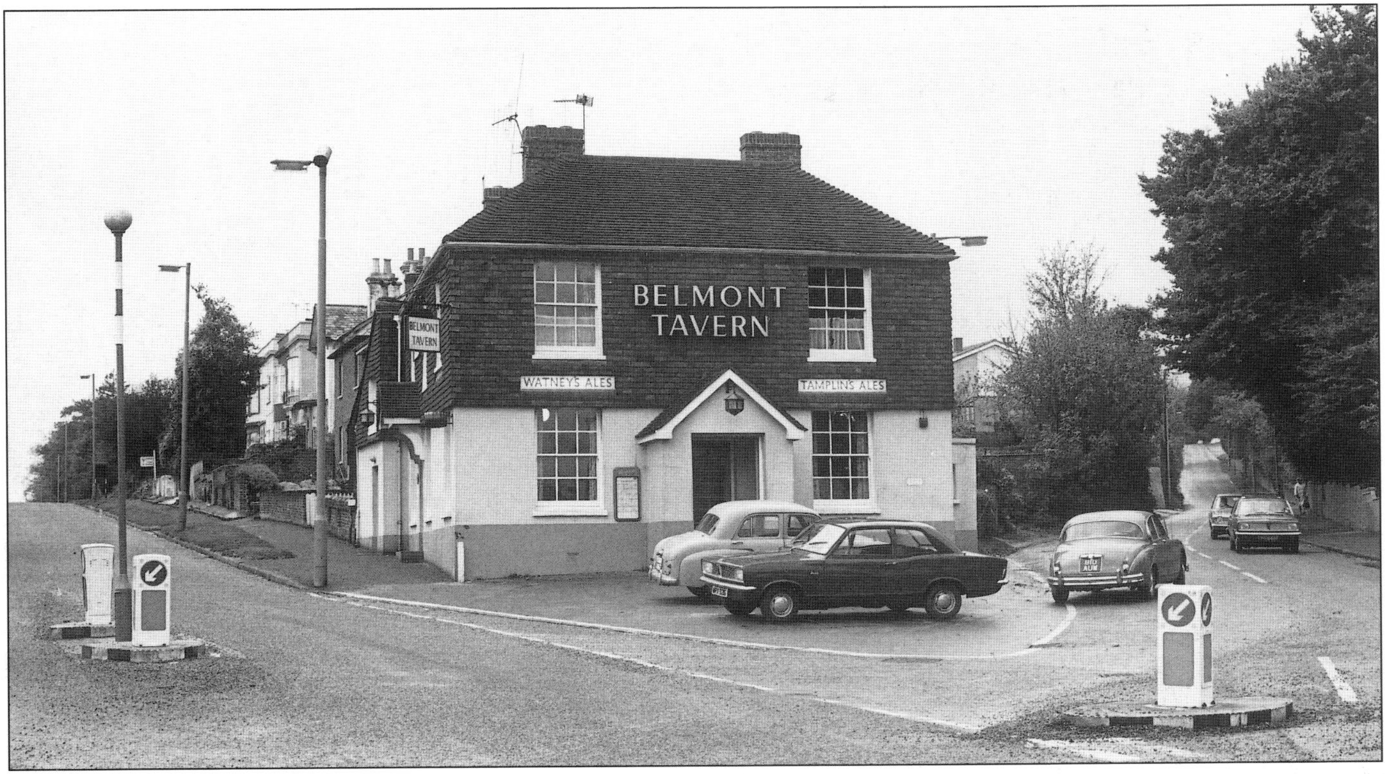

The road starts to climb up the hill to the right of the old Belmont Tavern at Bedhampton. The inn was demolished and its successor was built just across the road.

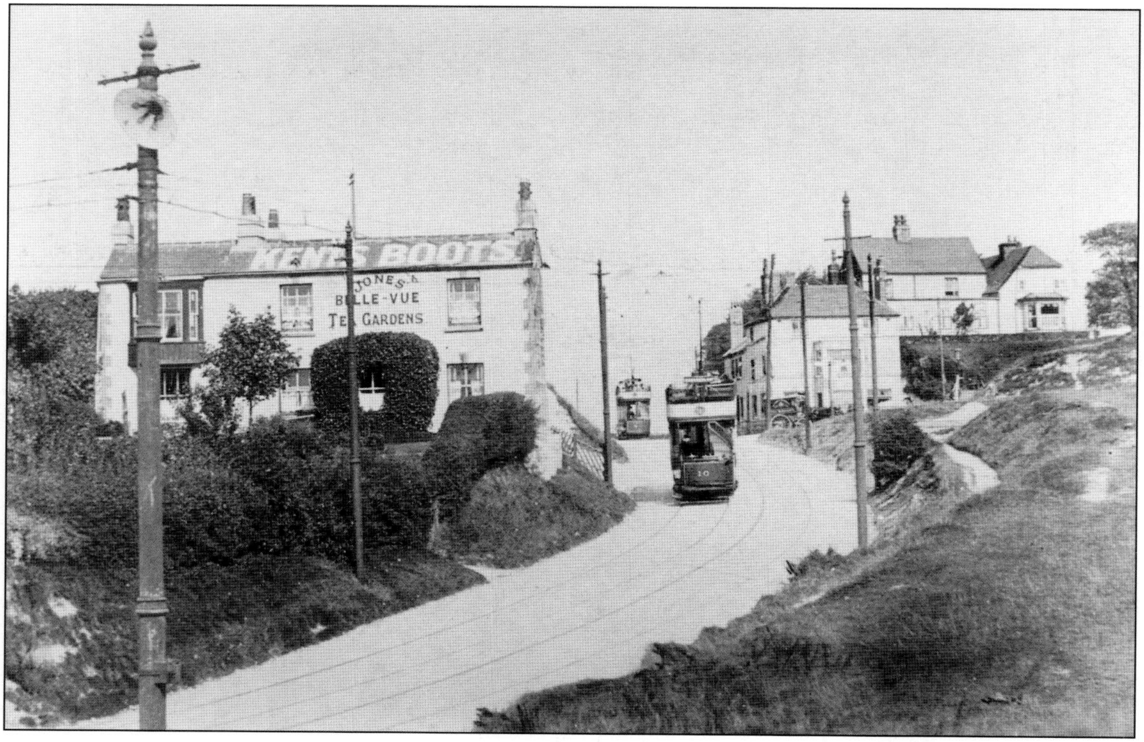

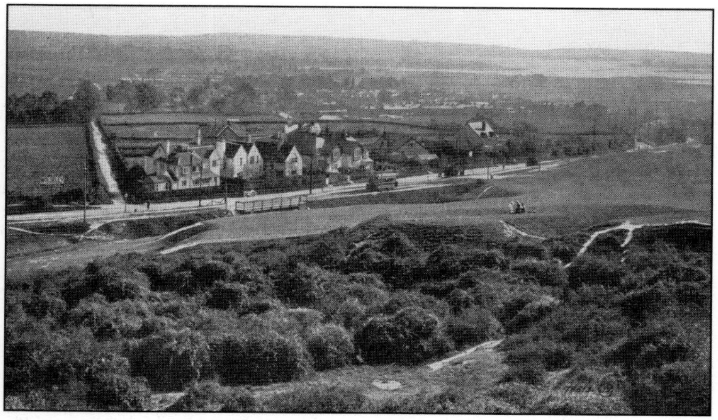

Above: *Two trams of the Portsdown and Horndean Light Railway prepare to pass each other at the crossroads in those quieter days at the beginning of the last century. The tramway was opened on 2 March, 1903, and ran from Cosham to Horndean. The George Inn is on the right of the picture, with behind it, The Cottage, the home of Alfred White who was managing director and chief engineer of the company. The house was fed with power from the tramway's DC system, which meant that when the trams stopped running for the night, the oil lamps and candles came into use in the White household.*

Left: *A tram makes its way towards what was officially called Point A, where passengers travelling on Portsmouth trams would change to join the Portsdown and Horndean Light Railway. A flight of concrete steps still marks the spot today.*

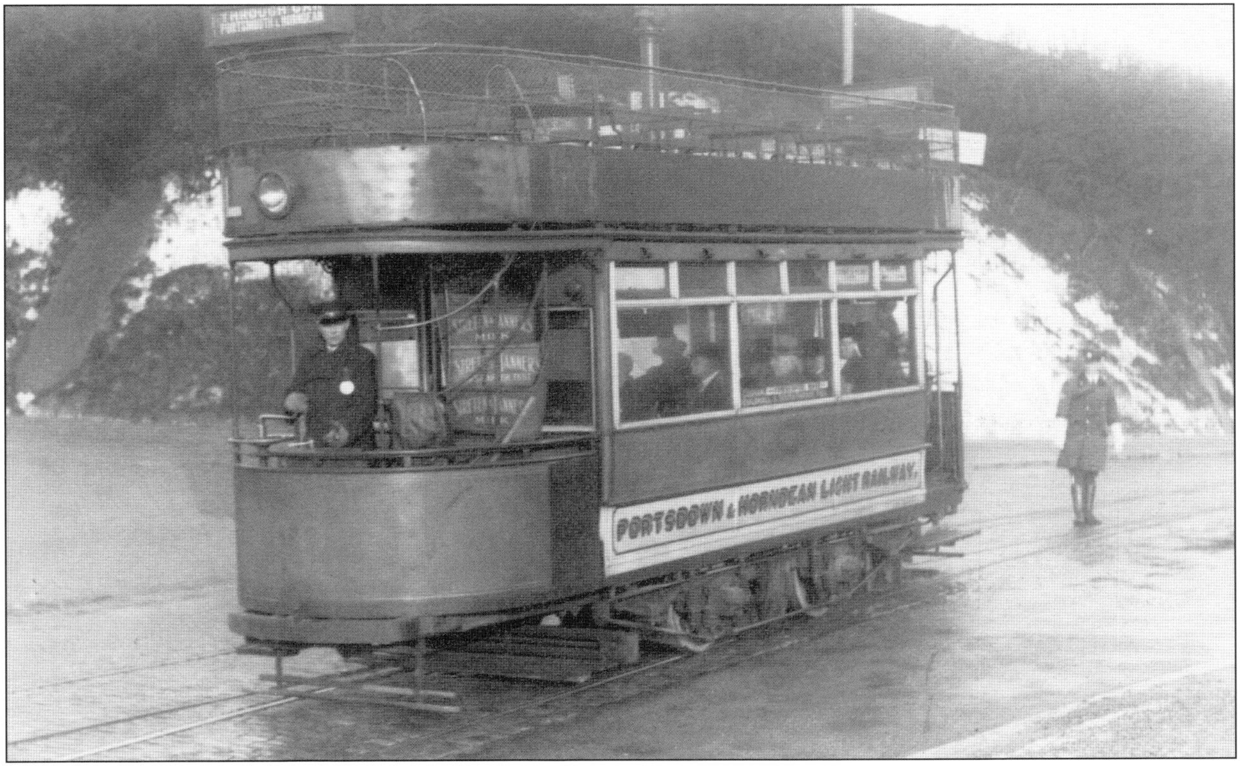

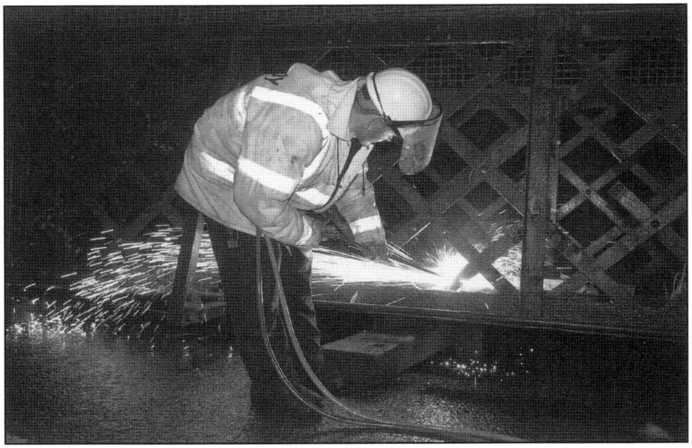

Above: *The advent of the silent service – the trolleybuses – brought an end to the Portsmouth trams and to the light railway. On the last day, 9 January 1935, motorman Fred Wells brings the last Horndean car over the brow of the hill on its final journey.*

Right: *On a cold December morning in 2000, before it was even light, workmen began the task of removing the old footbridge from across the lower part of Southwick Hill Road, removing the last major reminder of the Portsdown and Horndean Light Railway.*

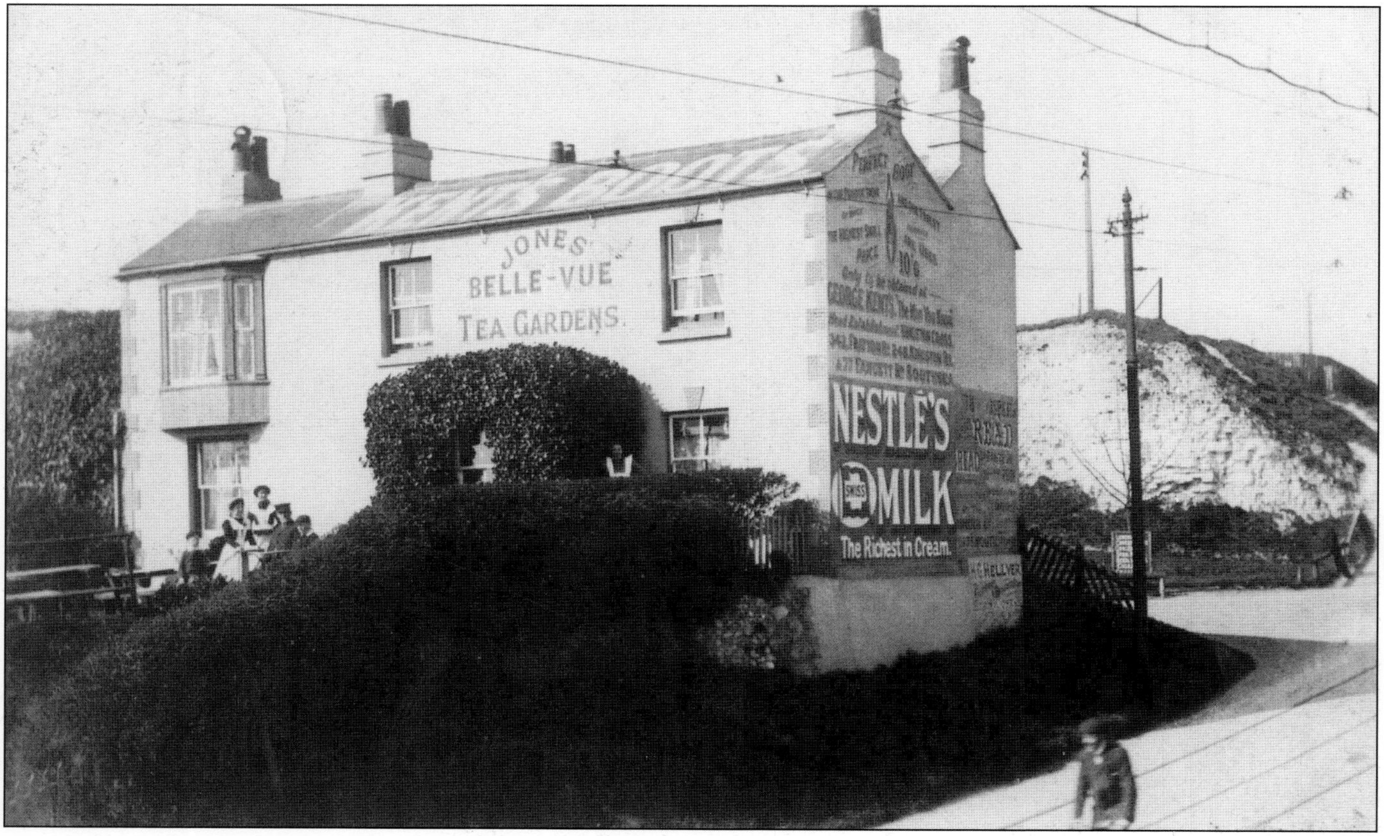

A popular place at the summit of the hill to break the tram journey to Horndean was Jones's Tea Rooms, a business that seemed to thrive on advertising revenue, especially that of George Kent whose boot-making emporium was based in Kingston Crescent.

The tea gardens provided everything that was needed for an enjoyable stop. A waitress lays a table while a customer awaits her order. What looks suspiciously like a redundant railway carriage or tram can be seen at the left of the picture.

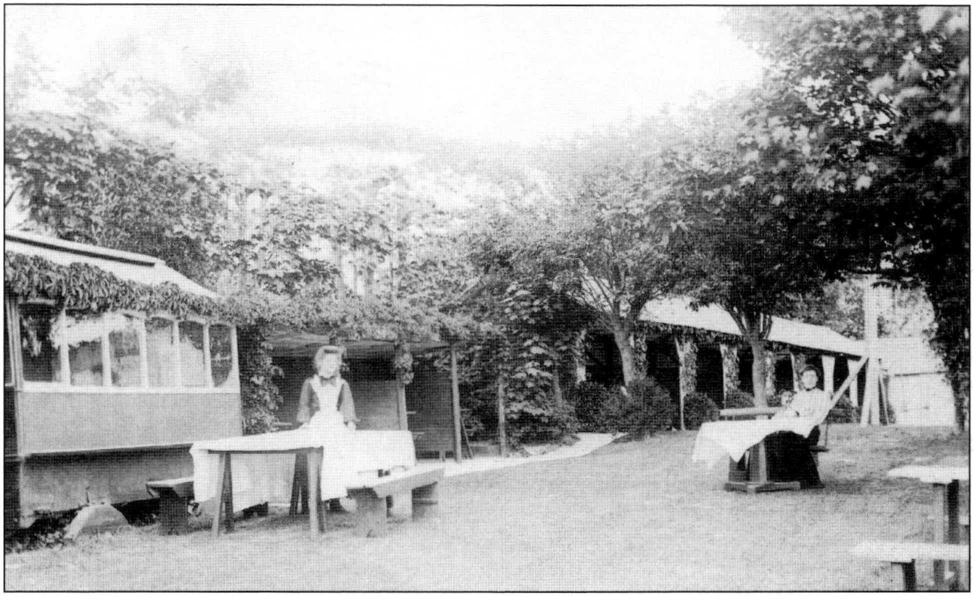

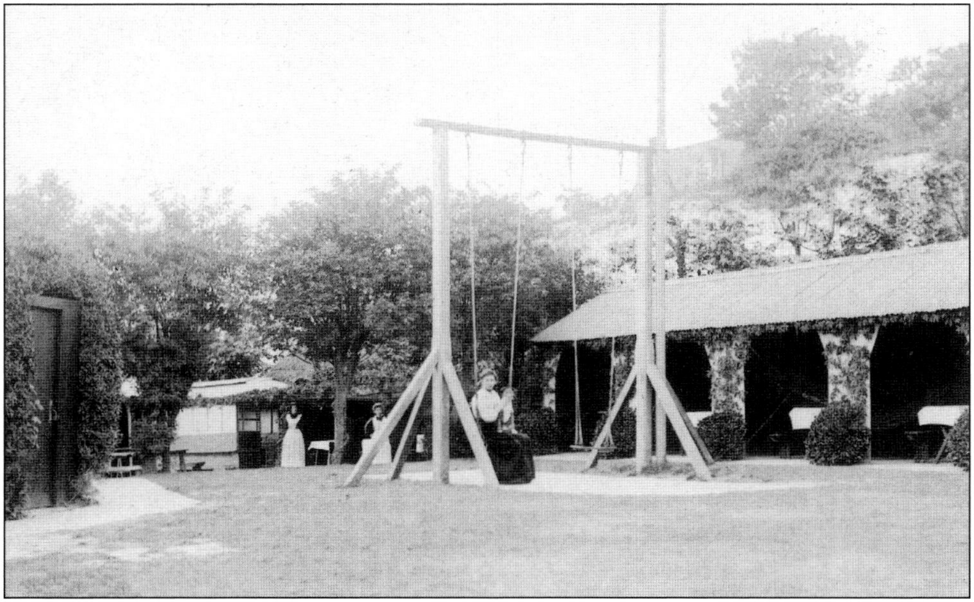

Perhaps it wasn't just the children that took to the swings as this obviously posed picture shows. Two waitresses watch the photographer, while the neatly laid tables in the outdoor booths await patrons.

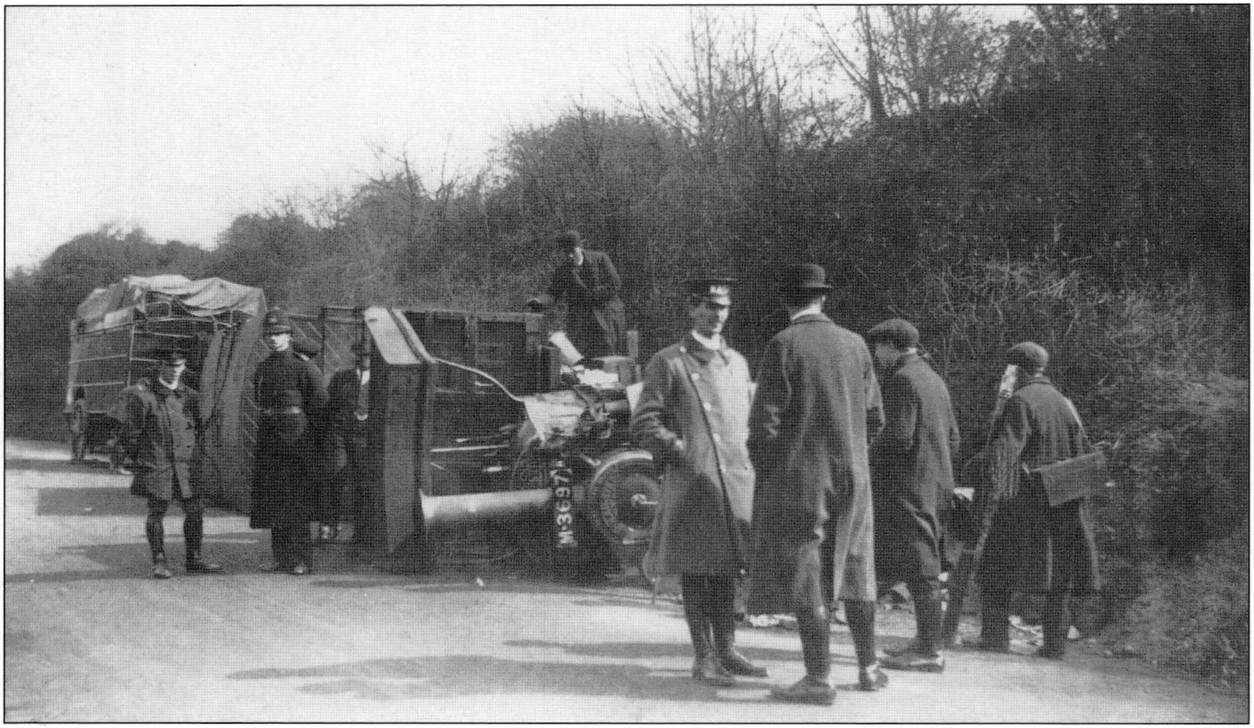

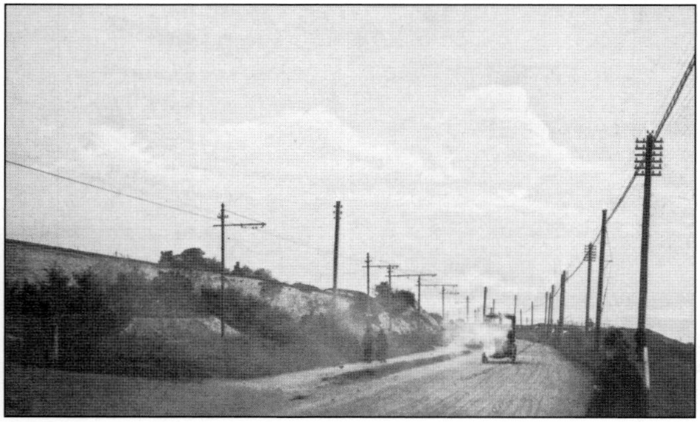

Above: *Road accidents are not necessarily a problem brought on by today's fast and powerful cars. On Tuesday 24 March 1914, an unfortunate traction engine driver named Henry Simpson lost control of his vehicle, driving it on to the grass bank where it turned over. Mr Simpson, from Lower Edmonton, was taken to the Royal Hospital in Portsmouth, suffering from a fractured skull and a broken arm. In August 1938 a coach carrying day-trippers from Guildford skidded on the hill and crashed, leaving more than 30 passengers injured. At the time it was the worst road accident to have occurred within the city boundaries.*

Left: *A puff of exhaust smoke indicates a gear change for this early car as it makes its way up the hill towards the George crossroads.*

In 1940 much of southern England suffered the coldest January since 1814, when even the Thames froze. Britain was deep in wartime censorship and even the newspapers could not report on the bad weather for fear of providing useful information to the enemy. Cold rain hit the already frozen ground and immediately covered everything in a shiny glaze. These bus conductors and drivers were unable to take their vehicles down the hill into Portsmouth, so had to remain at the George on the summit.

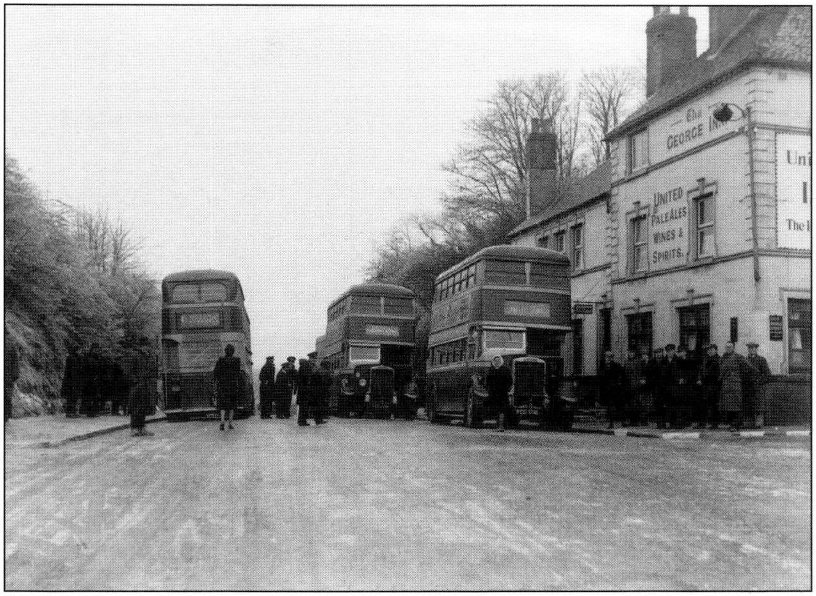

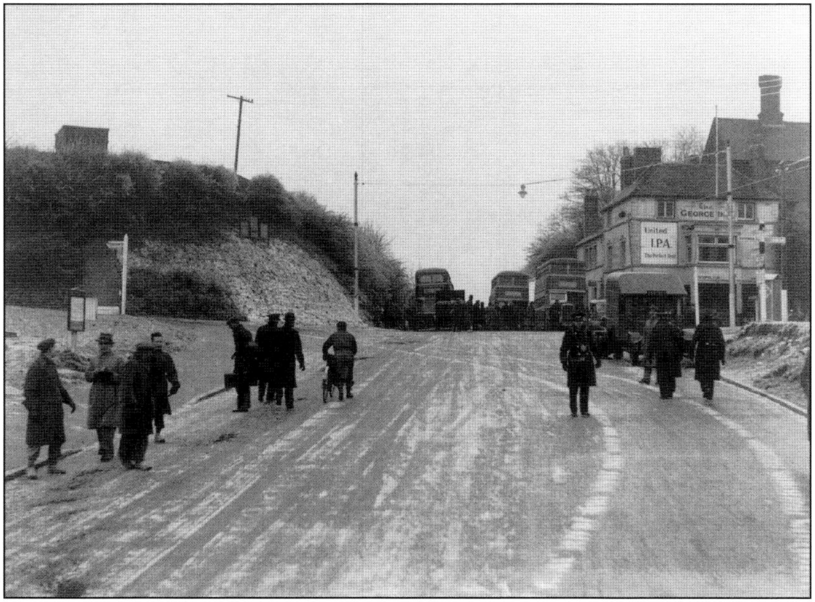

A cyclist and other pedestrians join cold bus company staff members, who are waiting out the weather at the top of the hill.

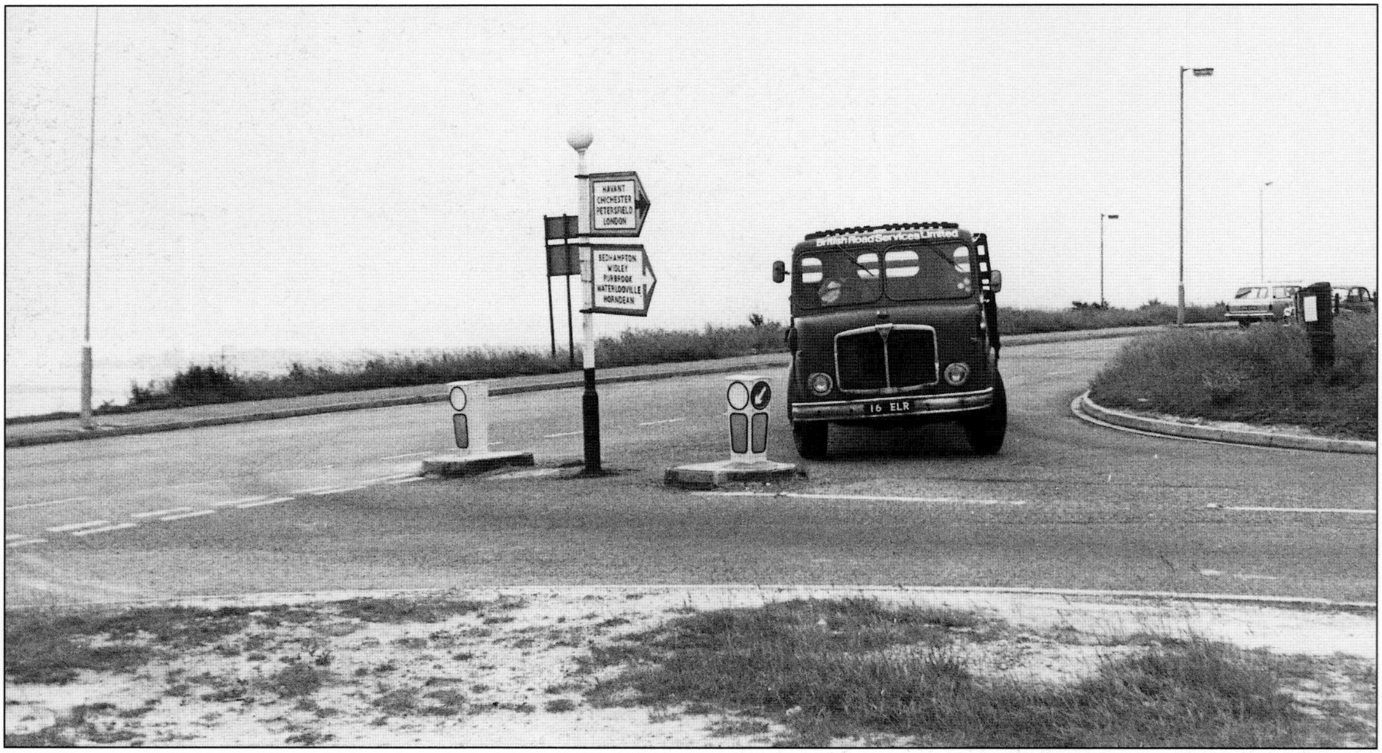

Traffic from a later era take things more sedately at the top of the hill in this simple photograph of a British Road Services truck from 1971.

As the years went by more people could afford cars and road traffic became much more heavy, so much so that a policeman on point duty was a permanent sight at the George crossroads.

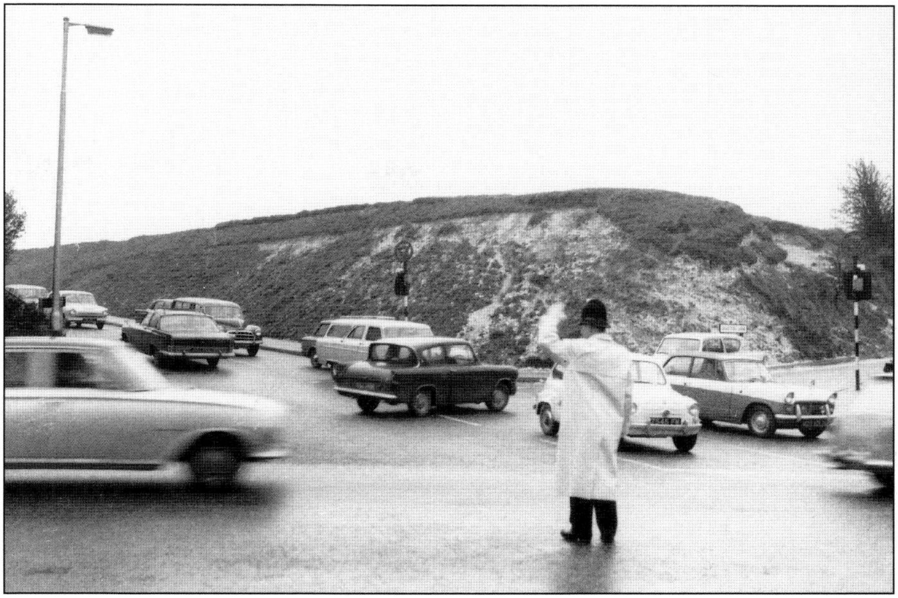

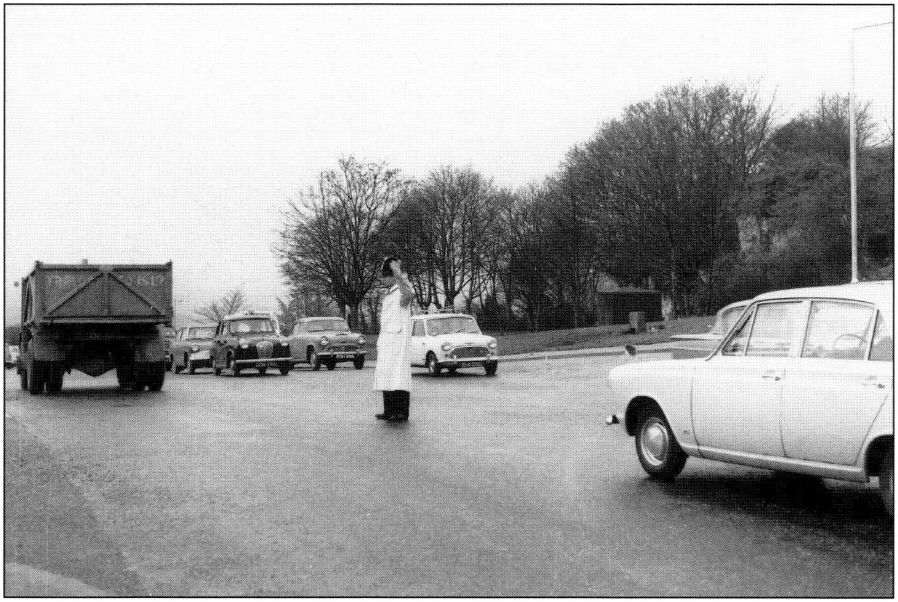

A selection of cars from yesteryear awaits the signal to move off on the summit of Portsdown.

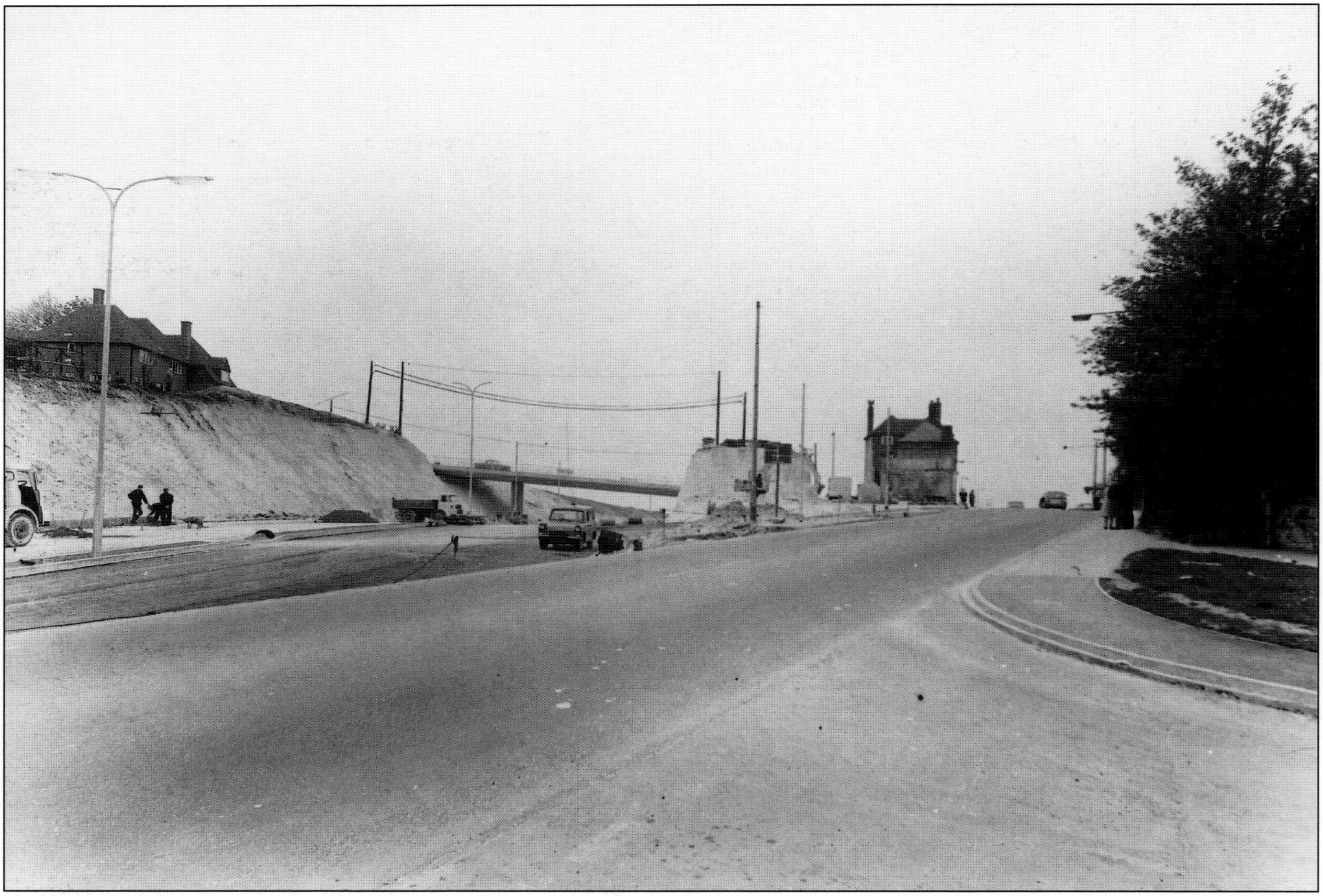

Eventually the city council put a huge road-widening project in place that entailed the construction of new roads and bridges.

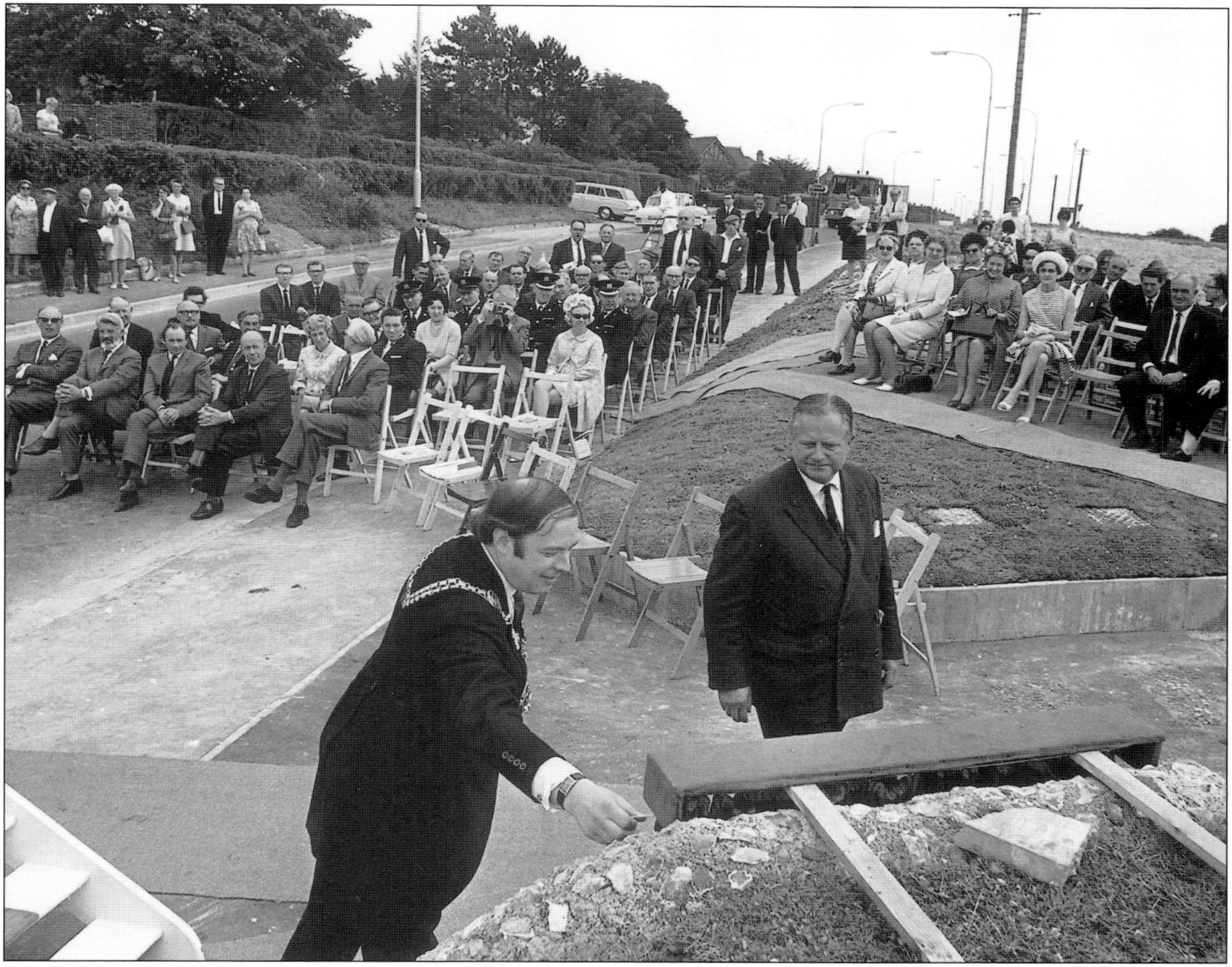

The new roads complex was opened on 19 July, 1968, by the then Lord Mayor of Portsmouth, Councillor Freddie Emery-Wallace, who unveiled a plaque to mark the occasion.

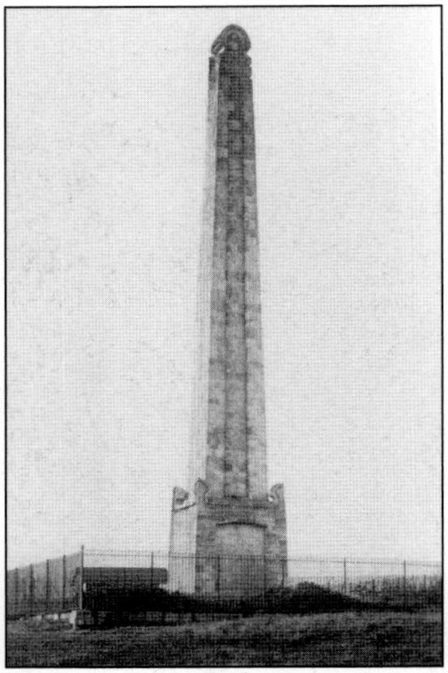

Left: *Following the death of Nelson at Trafalgar and to mark the famous admiral's successes, the first Nelson's Column – designed by John Thomas Groves – was erected on Portsdown Hill, every sailor donating a day's pay to fund it. The foundation stone of the hilltop landmark was laid on 4 July 1807, easily beating the famous London column, which wasn't completed until 1843. In 1899 it was discovered that much of the stonework was crumbling so the column was pulled down with just the base left intact. The outer walls were rebuilt in Portland stone and the interior was filled with concrete. The top eight-foot section had the original stone replaced, and the bust of Nelson – which is hollow – was set back in position. The task was completed in February 1900.*

Below: *The monument shows up clearly in this superb aerial view above Fort Nelson taken in the 1950s. Workmen are still working on the underground water reservoir which helps feed Portsmouth and surrounding villages.*

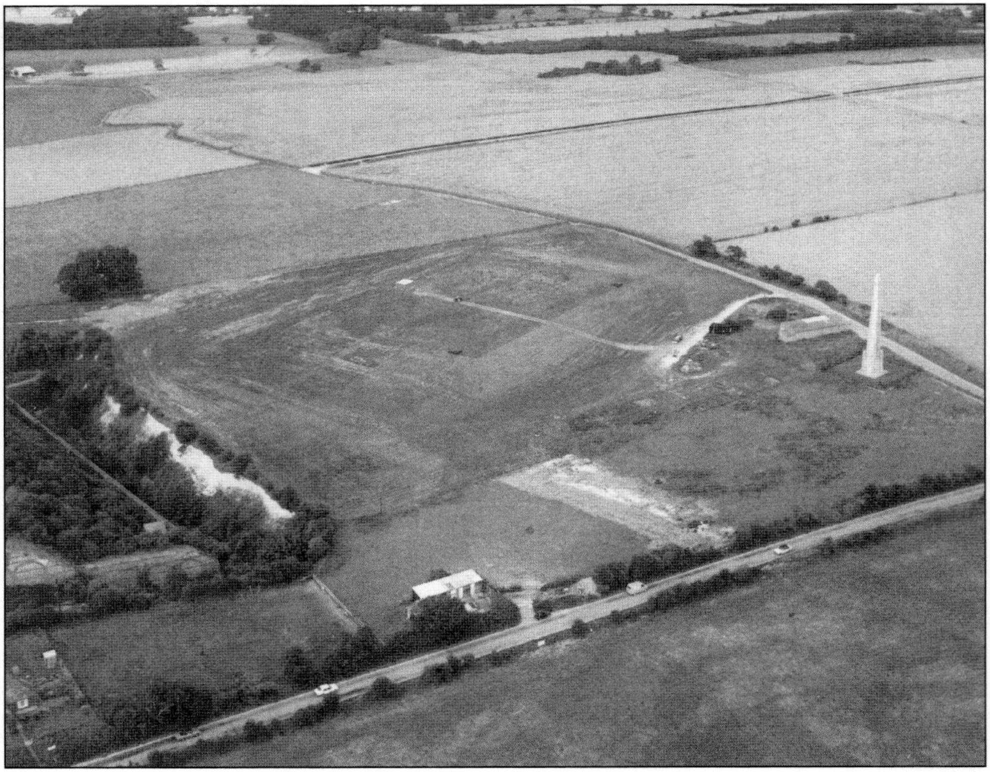

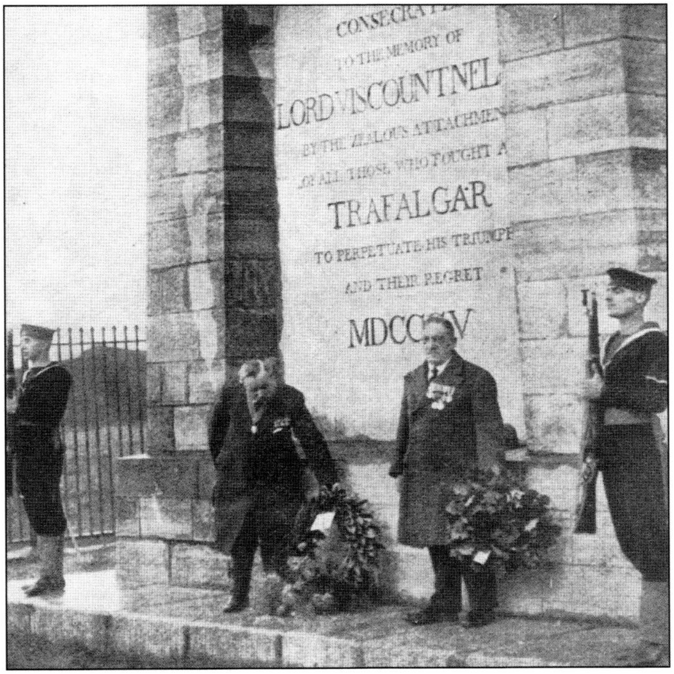

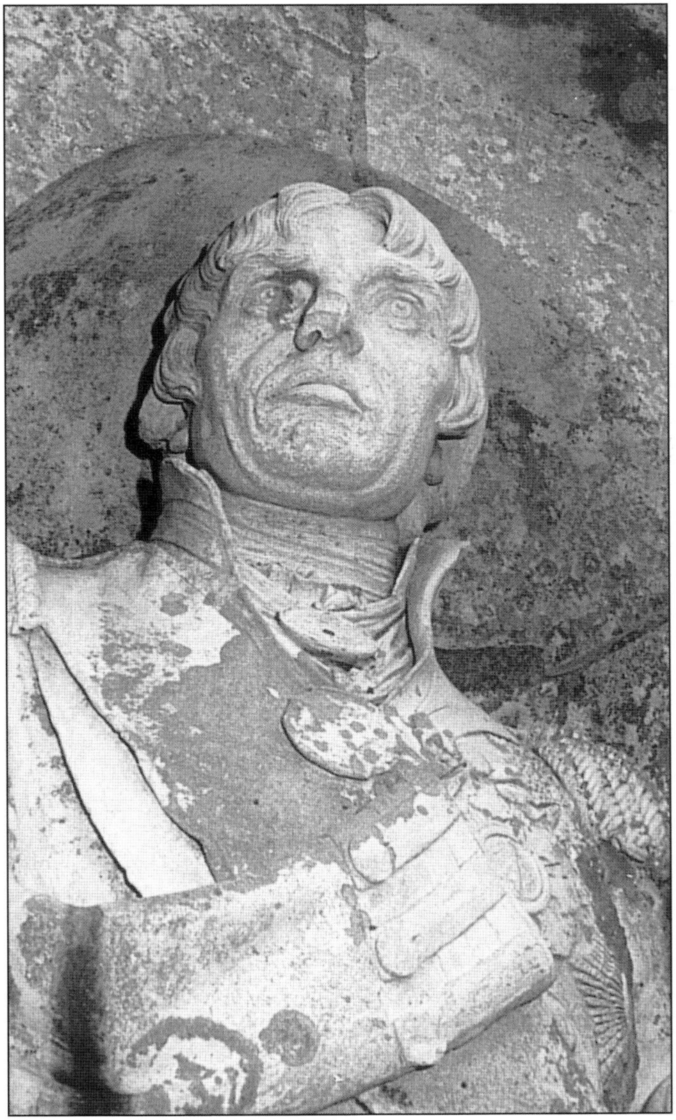

Above: *Trafalgar Day used to be marked at the Nelson monument with a wreath-laying ceremony, but nowadays this practice has been discontinued.*

Right: *A stony-faced Admiral Nelson looks down upon Portsmouth from his vantage point atop the pillar.*

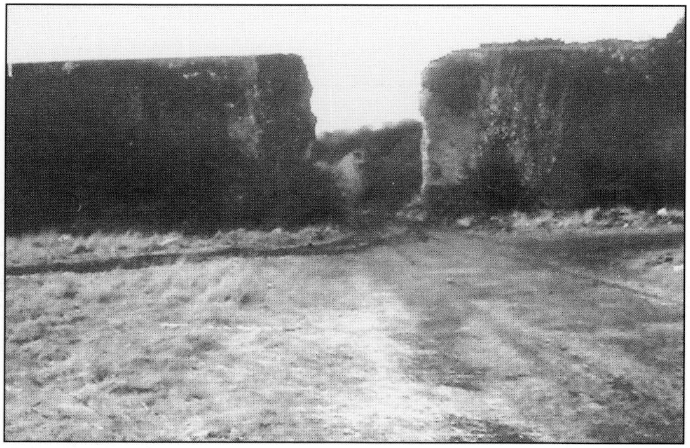

Left: *Fort Wallington was the smallest of the Portsdown forts. After the war the fort remained unused until 1961, when it was sold to a developer who demolished most of it in order to turn the site into an industrial estate. In this rare picture part of the outer wall is still standing. At one time the Dungeon Club was a popular meeting place deep below Fort Wallington.*

Below: *The year is 1989 and Fort Nelson is pictured from the air. Royal Armouries took over the fort and it is now a popular and interesting museum. Visitors coming to the fort today can see some of the huge examples of artillery displayed near the entrance, which were not in place when the helicopter did its flyby for this view.*

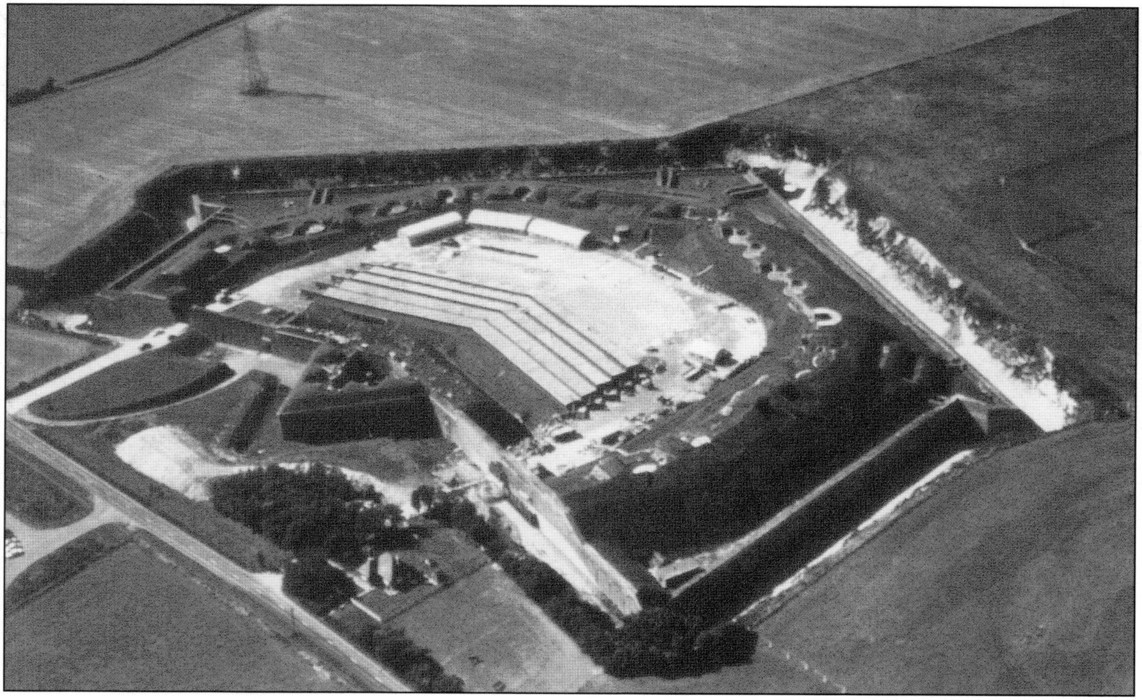

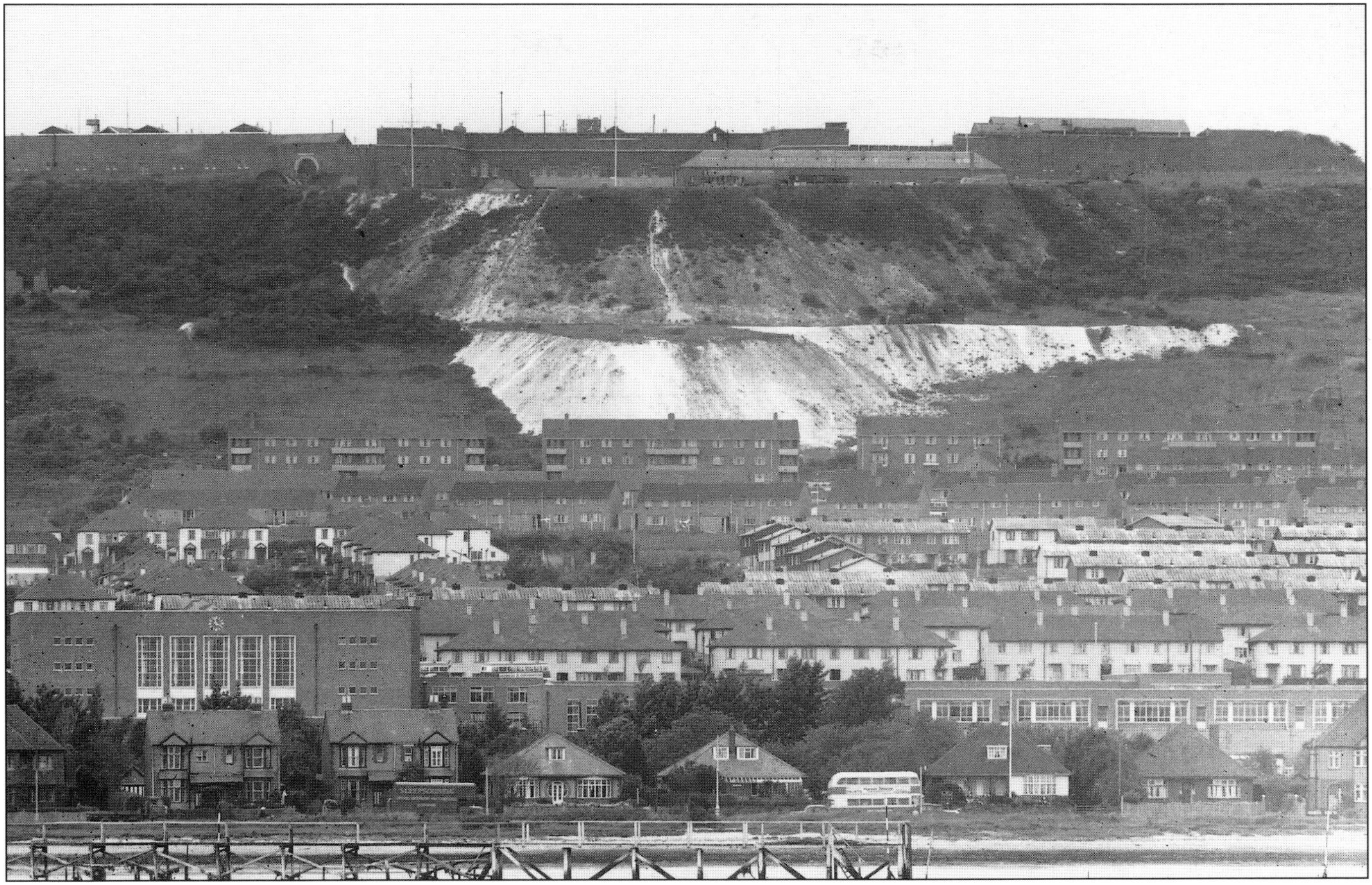

The camera has now moved eastwards to Fort Southwick which sits on the skyline in this view from down below on the A27. The huge chalk cliff – dumped there from the excavations of all the other forts – is clearly visible. In the lower part of the picture is King Richard School with its clock still in position high on the wall.

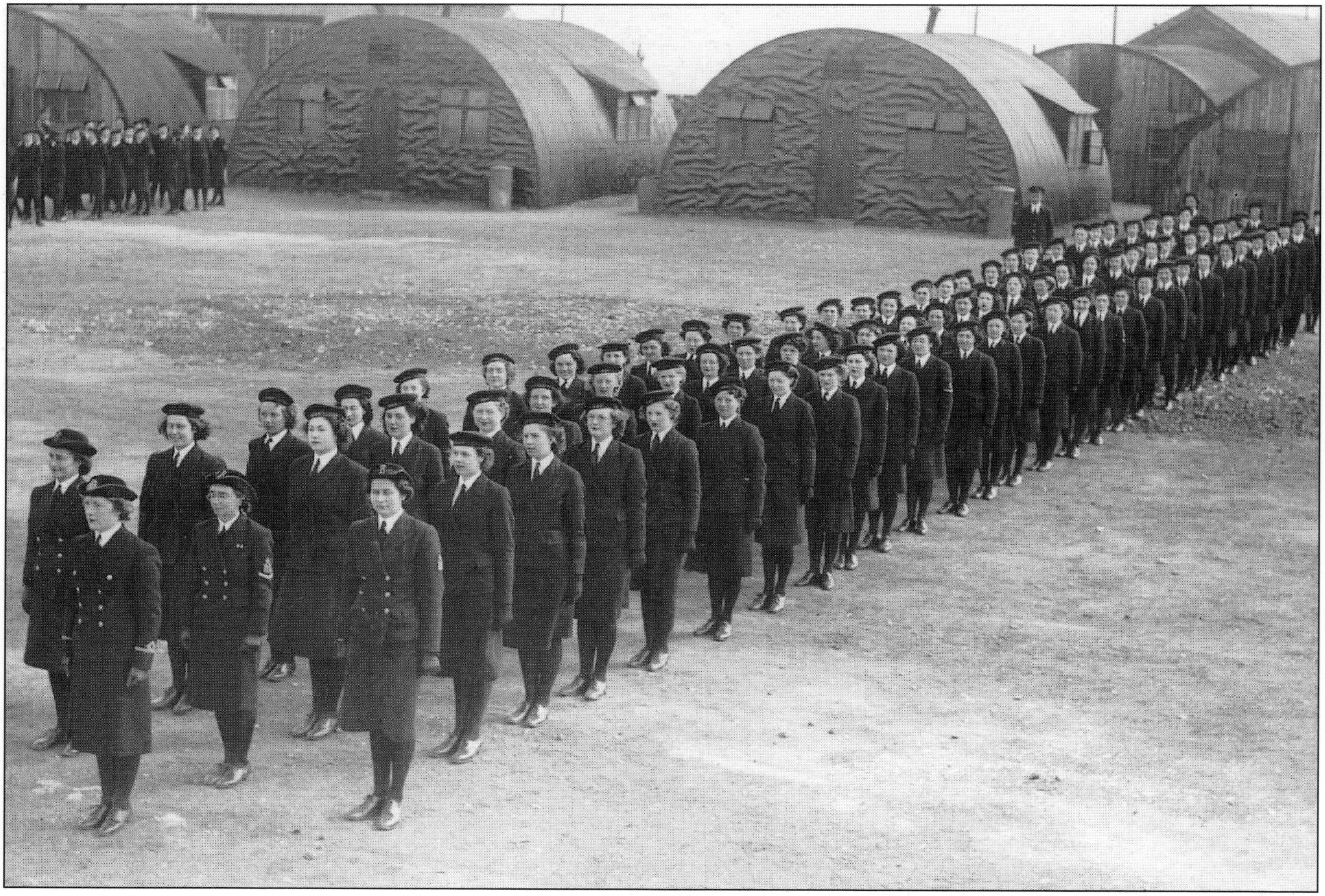

A smart group of Wrens are seen on parade at Fort Southwick, backed by temporary buildings erected for the duration of the war. During the Second World War an underground headquarters was constructed under the fort, which provided a bombproof control centre for the combined services designed to gather information in the build-up to D-Day. Radar and shipping information was co-ordinated in the huge plotting room before being passed to the Allied commanders at nearby Southwick House.

The Wrens take the salute at Fort Southwick, marching along what was the military road.

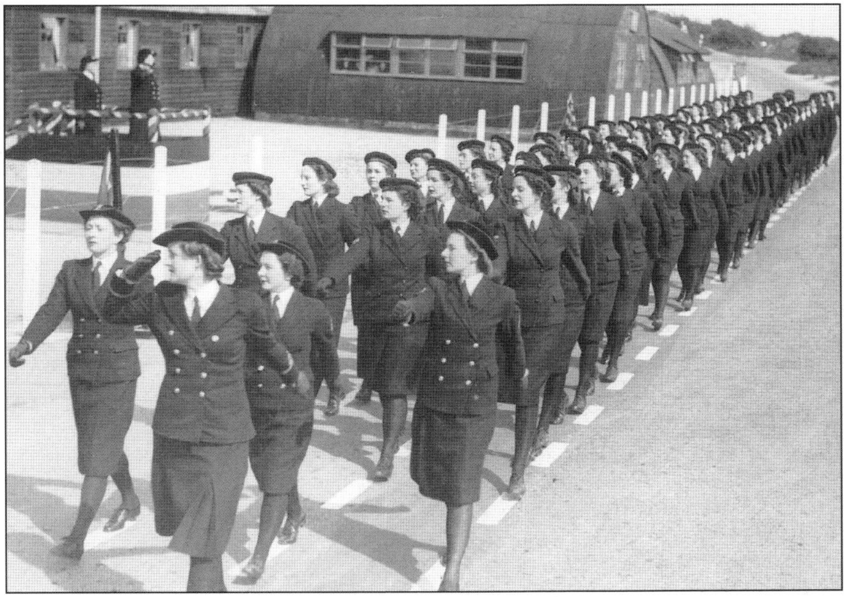

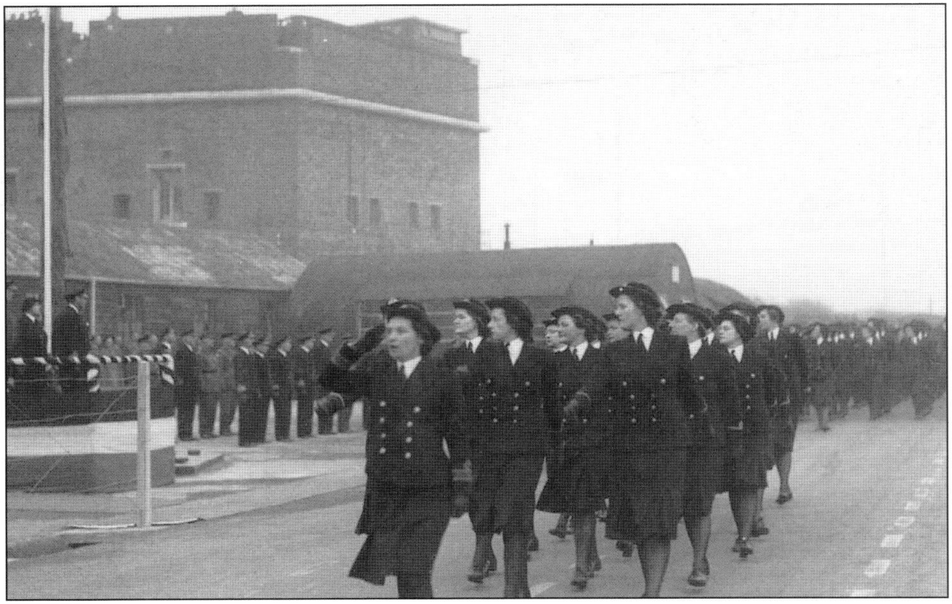

More Wrens take the salute, this time with the high wall of the fort in the background.

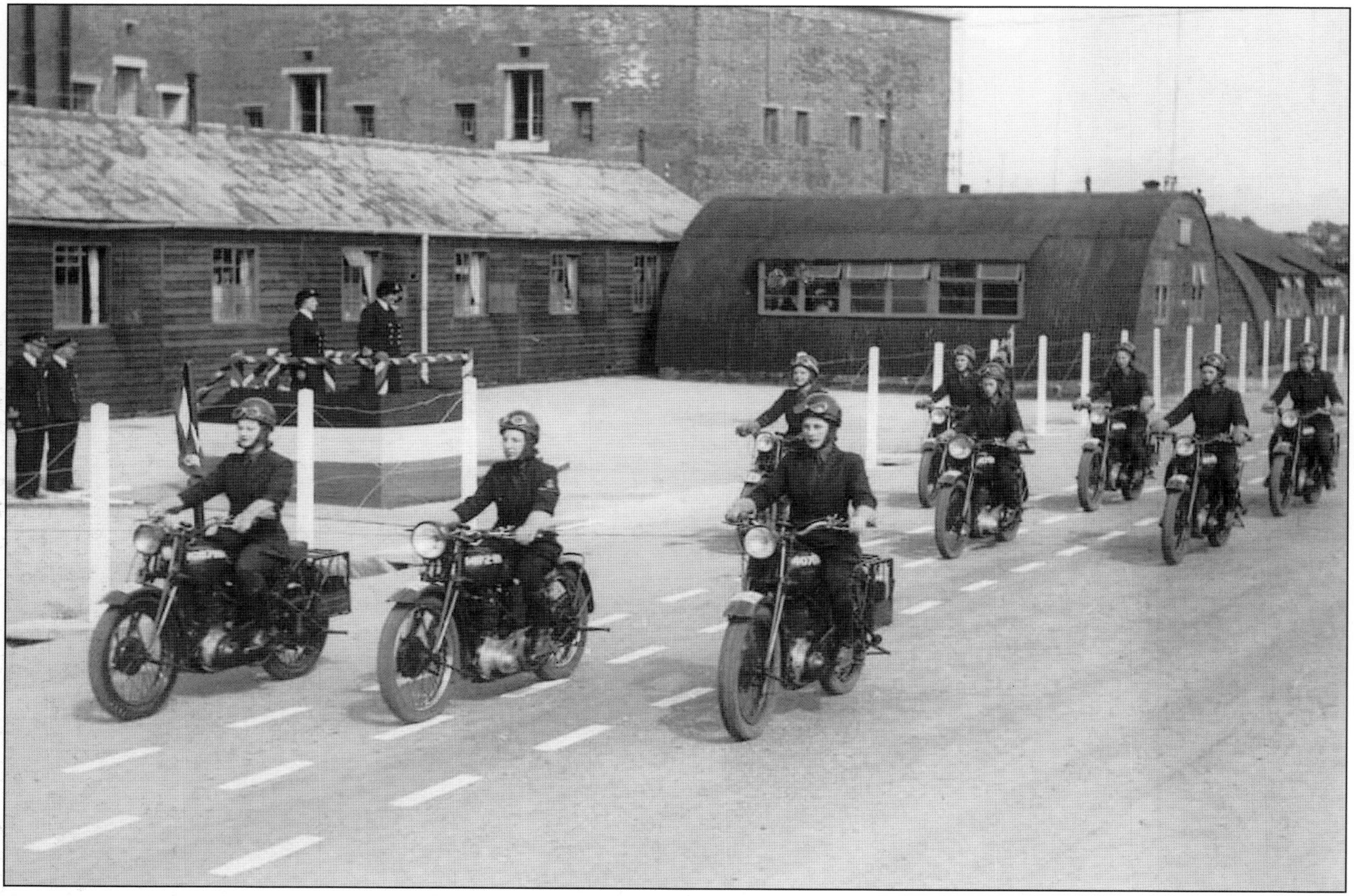

A different view of service life as motorised Wrens show their riding skills.

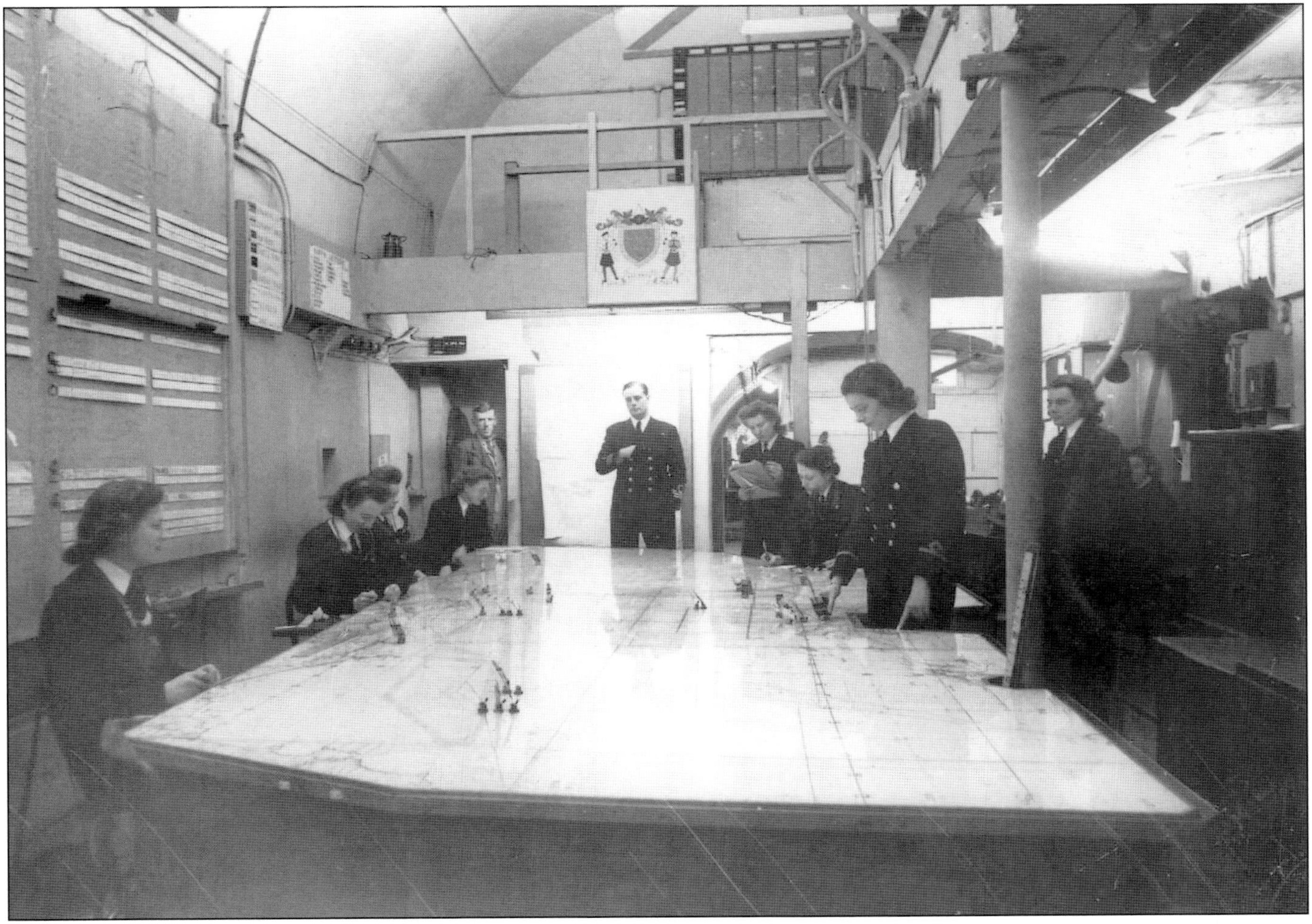

The plotting room in action, situated deep below in the 1 mile of Second World War tunnels below Fort Southwick.

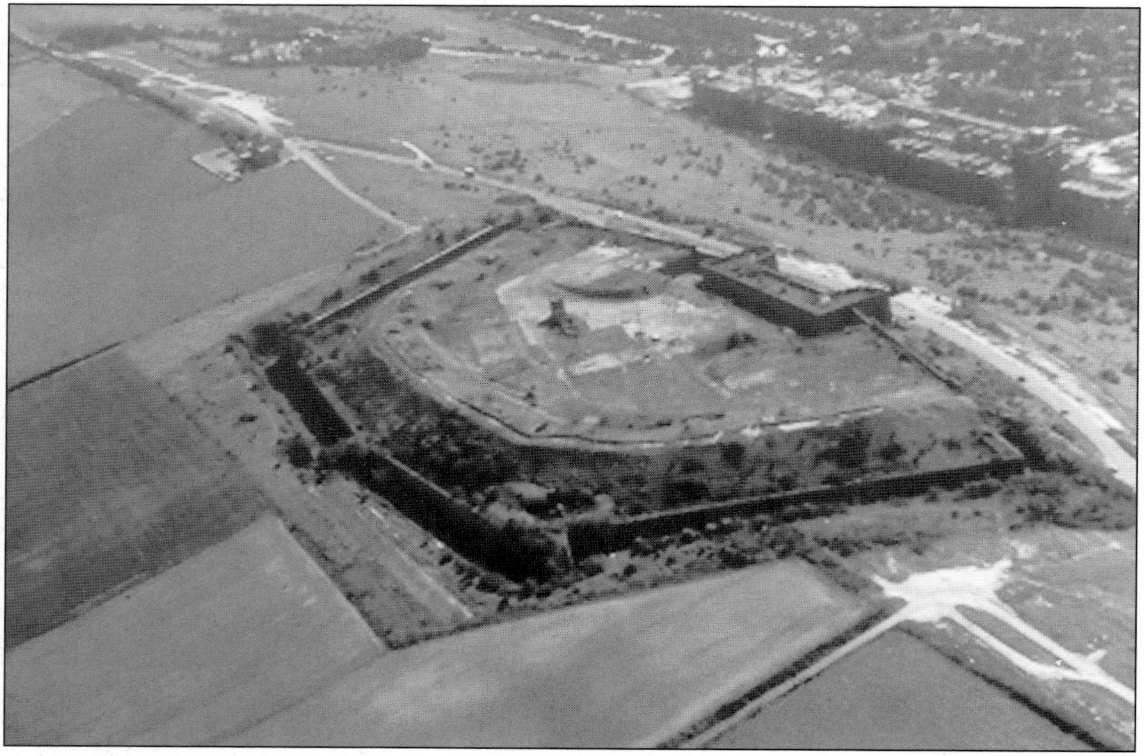

Fort Widley presents a stunning view from the air in this picture from the 1970s. Portsdown Park can clearly be seen at the top right of the picture.

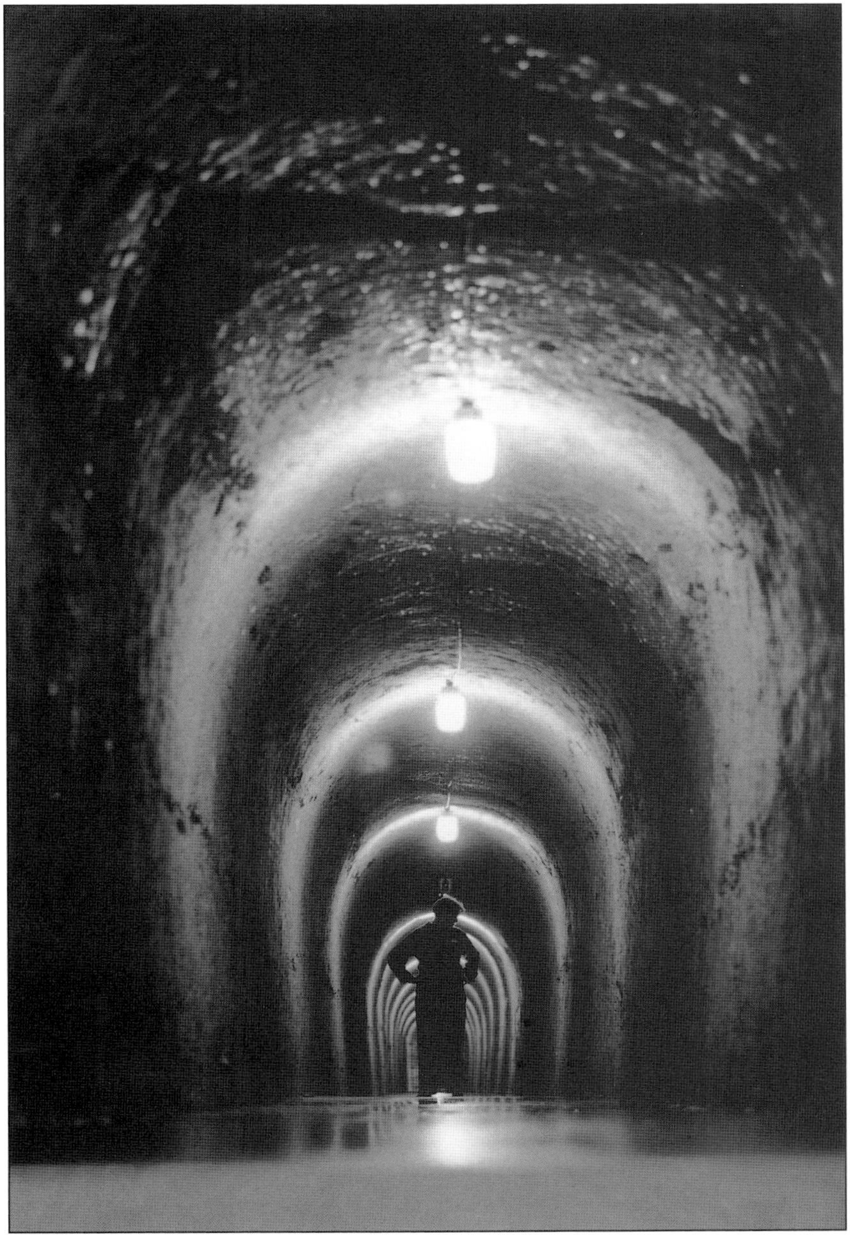

One of the original tunnels that run beneath Fort Widley taken in 1994 when the fort was open to visitors. Lower down the hill slopes, just off Southwick Hill Road, are Widley Cottages, originally the married quarters for fort personnel.

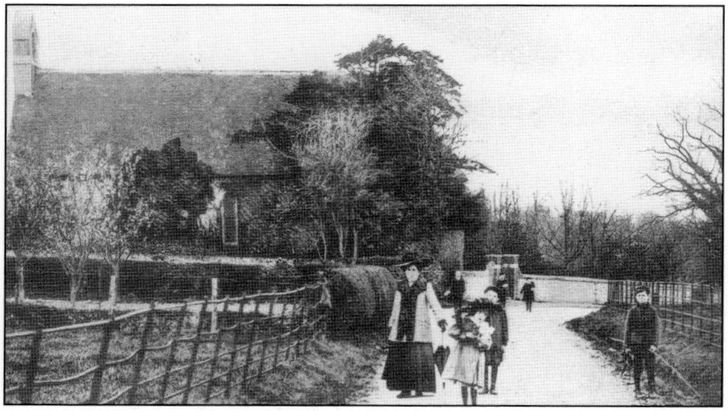

Left: *Fort Widley was named because it was built near the tiny village of Widley, which in mid Victorian times was situated just to the north of the fort. The village boasted a beautiful church which was built in 1850 and was eventually demolished in 1953. Present-day visitors can still see the graveyard and a small part of the church walls.*

Below: *In July 1995 Portsdown Hill, and Fort Widley in particular, became the location for the television series* Call Red. *Based on a helicopter rescue service, the crew and cast worked on this huge maze of scaffolding built around the eastern end of the fort. The series – aired between 8 January and 12 February 1996 – only lasted for five episodes, boasting such titles as* Invasion of the Body Snatchers, Baptism of Fire *and* Life Extinct. *In the foreground of this picture is the basket of the beacon lit on the hill to celebrate the Queen's Silver Jubilee in 1977.*

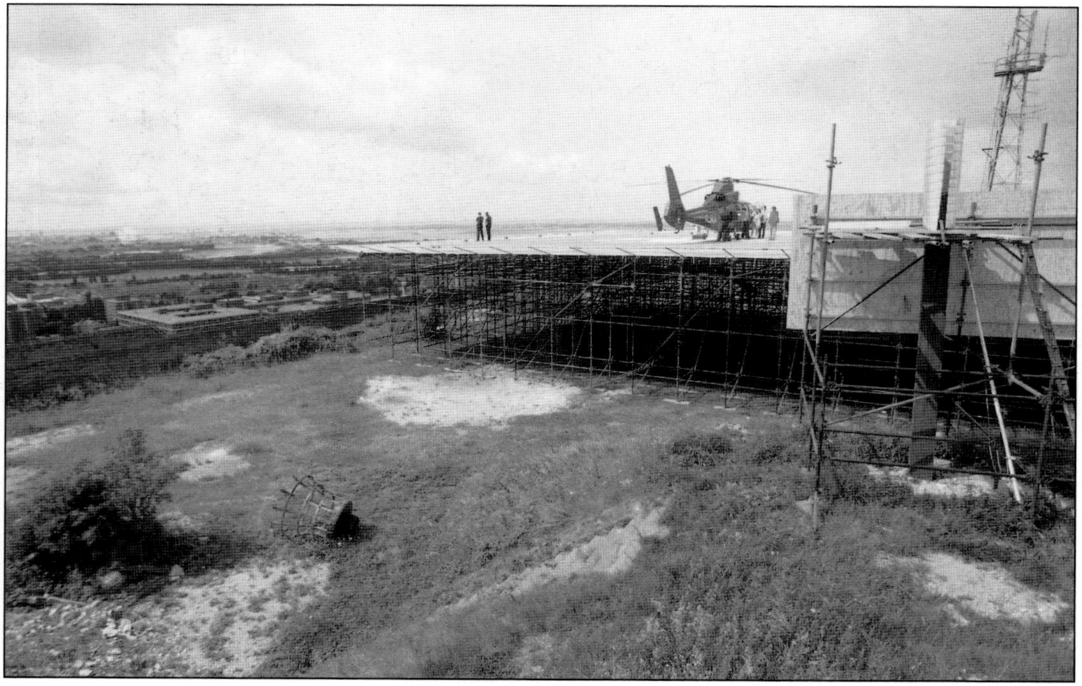

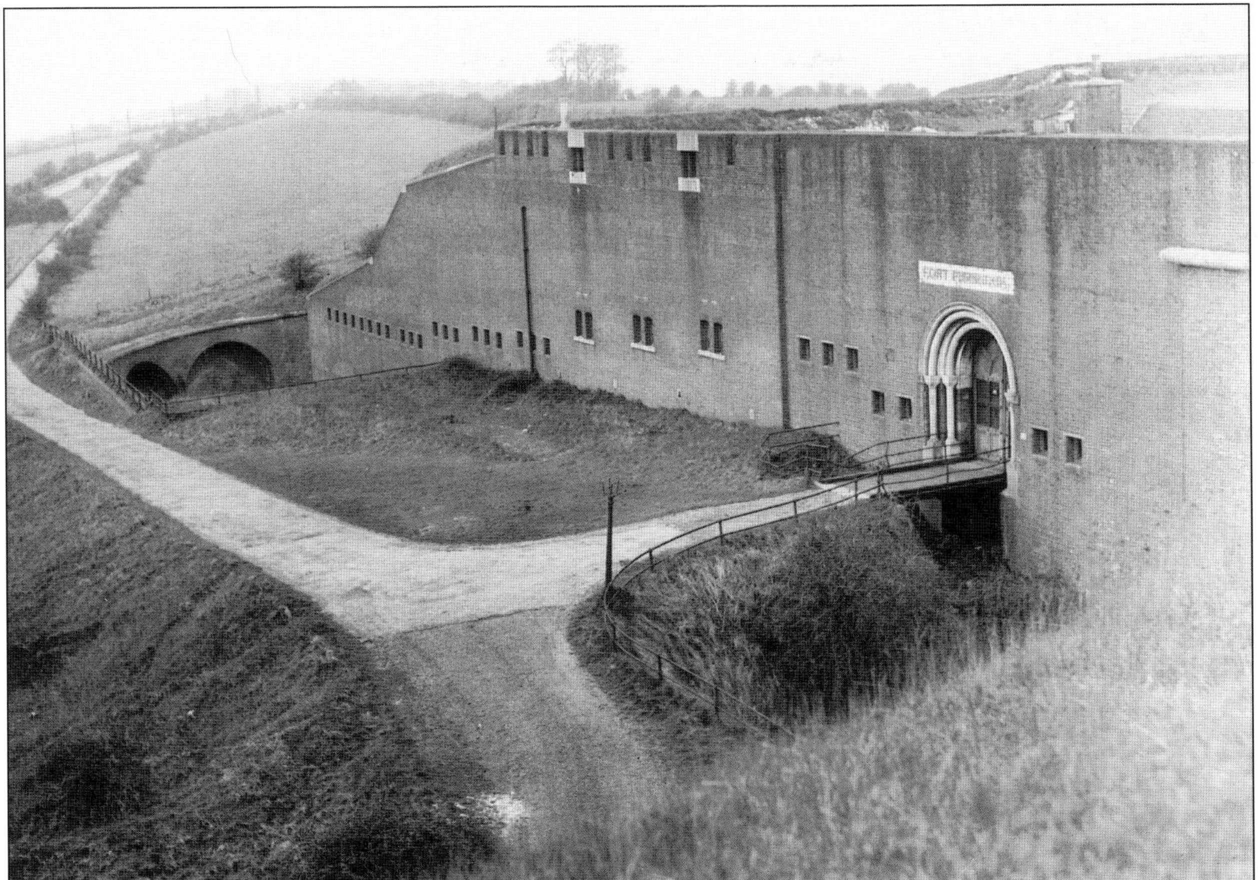

Fort Purbrook is the most easterly fort and is approximately 300 feet above sea level. Building commenced in 1862 and the construction was completed in about 1870. This picture was taken in the 1930s when the area around the fort presented a view so different to that of today.

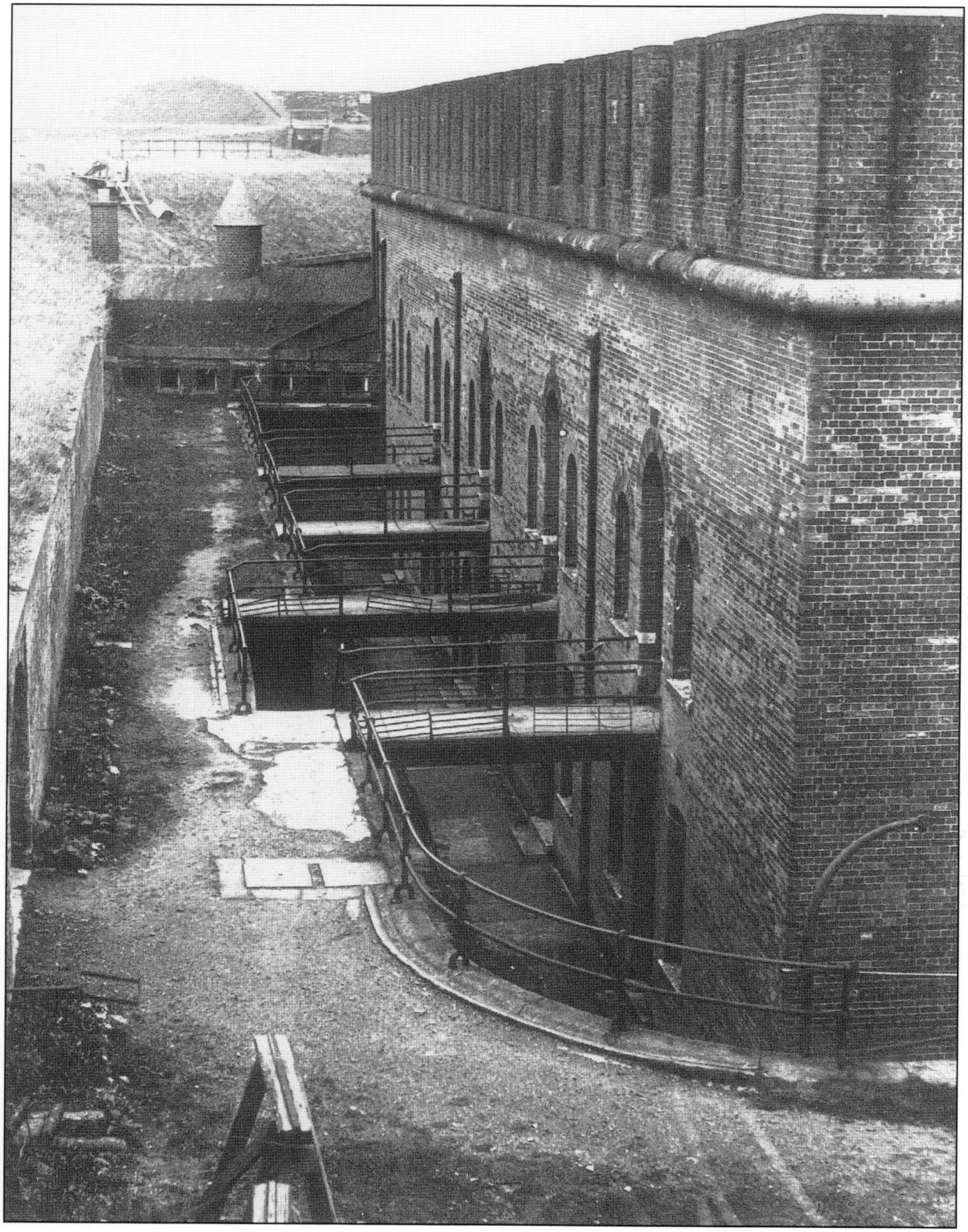

Taken at the same time as the previous picture, this photograph shows the rear of Fort Purbrook, with the protective ditch clearly visible. The complement of the fort was originally five junior officers, 227 other ranks, 20 hospital patients, and two horses.

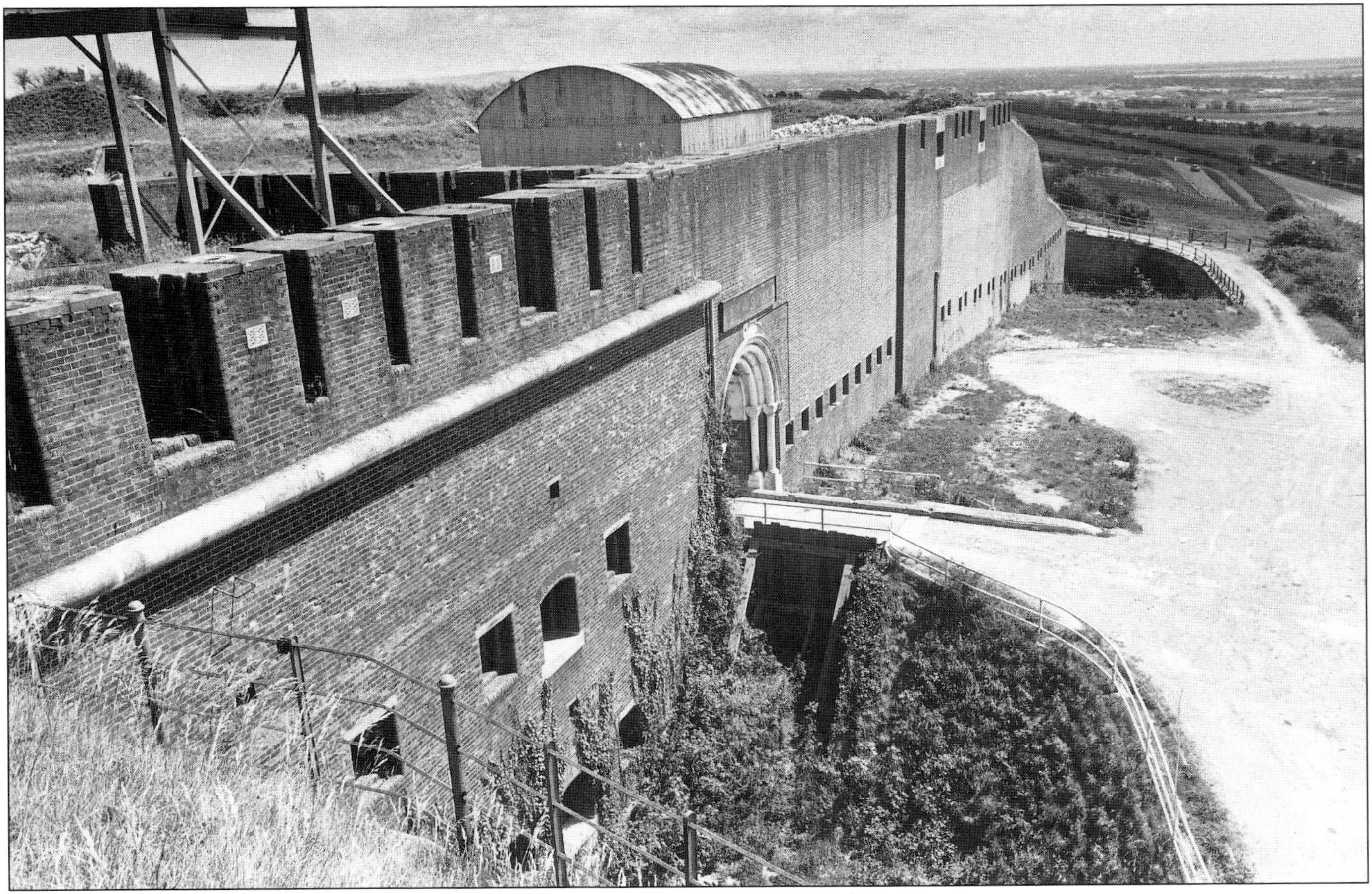

A different view of Fort Purbrook is seen here in this picture taken in 1972. Some of the temporary buildings, erected during the war, are still in position on the top of the fort. The fort was used as a location for the holiday camp scenes in the Ken Russell film Tommy.

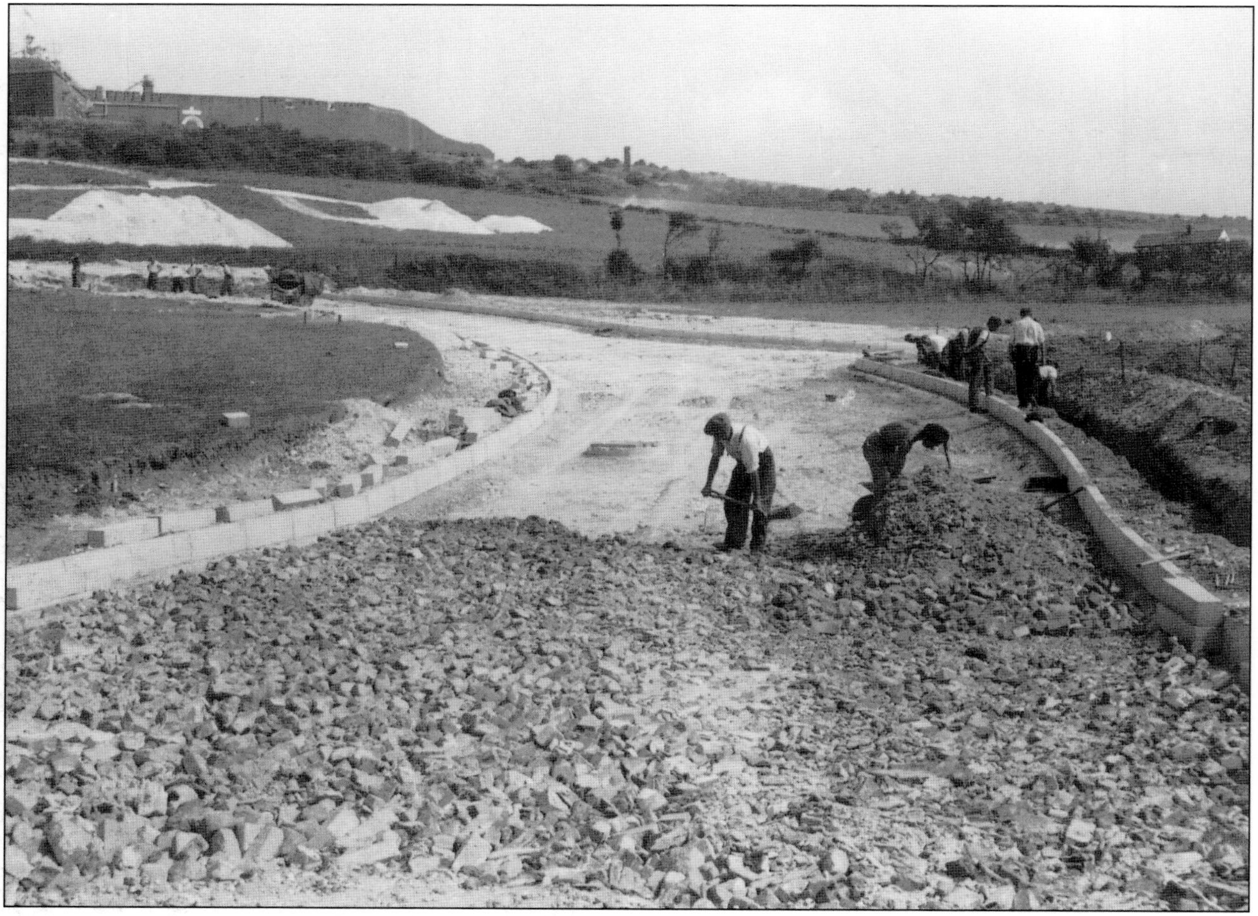

The year is 1955 and workmen are pictured here laying the foundations during the construction of Grant Road at Farlington. To the right of Fort Purbrook, in the background, is the chimney which was the air vent to one of the tunnels which ran from the fort to Farlington Redoubt.

Portsmouth City Council leased Fort Purbrook to the Portsmouth Youth Activities Committee and in November 1993 the then Lord Mayor of Portsmouth, Councillor Alex Bentley, opened the Peter Ashley Activity Centre, named in honour of the late city councillor.

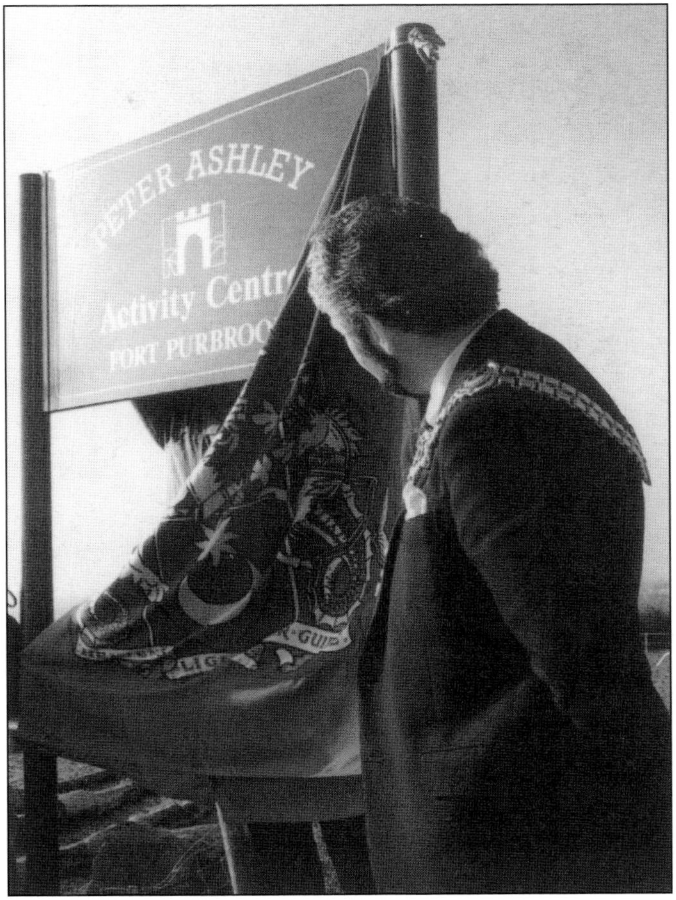

The estimated costs of the forts were:

Fort Wallington	*£100,569*
Fort Nelson	*£78,649*
Fort Southwick	*£94,262*
Fort Widley	*£93,980*
Fort Purbrook	*£135,000*

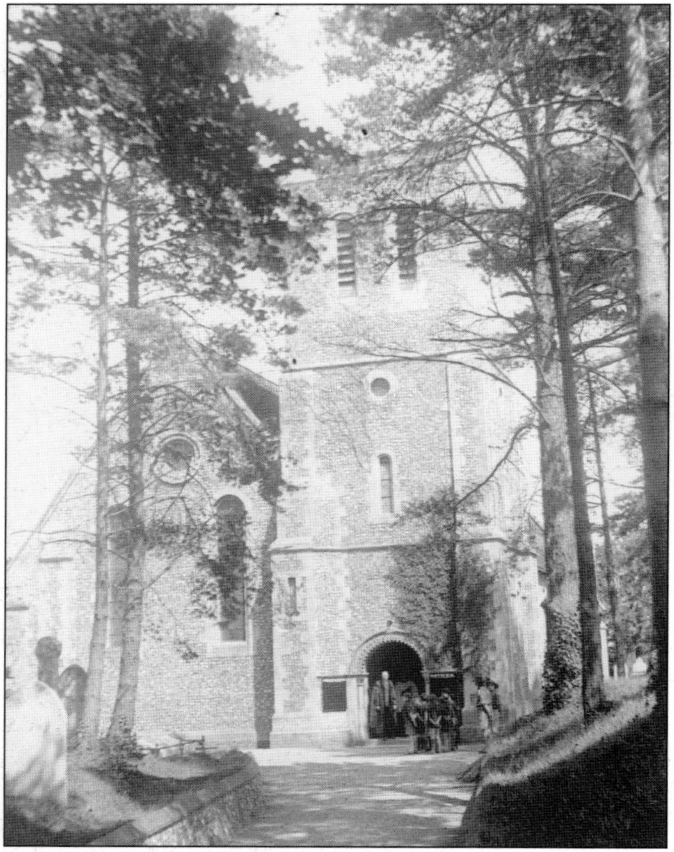

In 1860 the War Department purchased the land on Portsdown Hill to build the forts, much of which belonged to John Deverall, the Lord of the Manor of Farlington. The Secretary of State for War granted a one-acre site to build a church, which Deverall agreed to finance. The idea was to provide a place of worship for the servicemen who would be based at the forts. In return for the land the army was given rights to hold services in the church and to hold military burials if necessary. The church – pictured here in 1935 – was called Christ Church, Portsdown, and was consecrated on 30 July 1874.

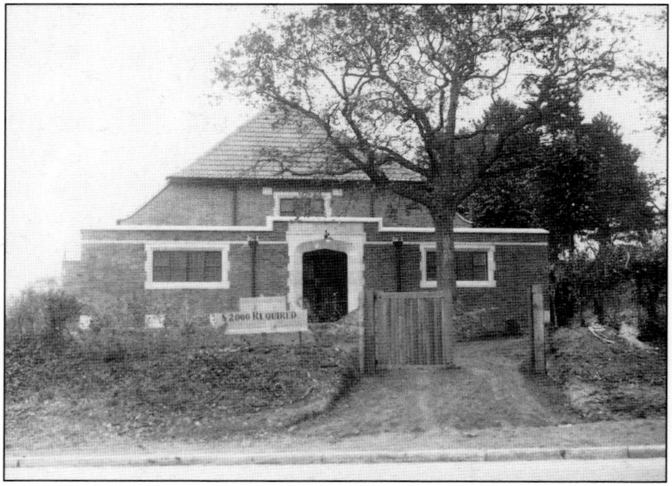

Fund-raising for the new church hall is obviously under way at Christ Church. According to the sign seen in this picture from 1935, £2000 is still required.

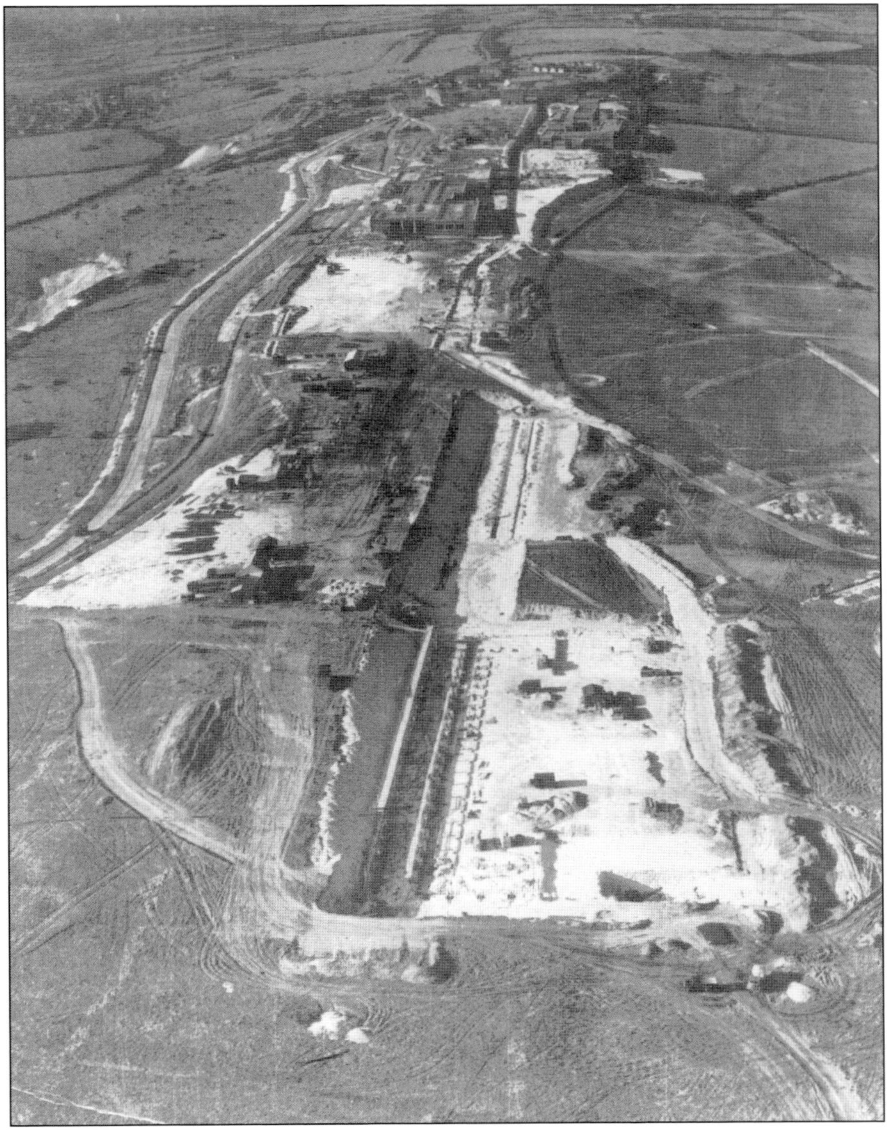

Surely one of the most distinctive buildings on the summit of the hill must be Portsdown Main. This aerial view from 1950 shows the Ministry of Defence site clearly with some of the first laboratories in position. At the bottom left is the old track which ran from Wymering to Southwick, and top left is the old ridgeway road, which now runs through the complex, with the new present-day road to its left.

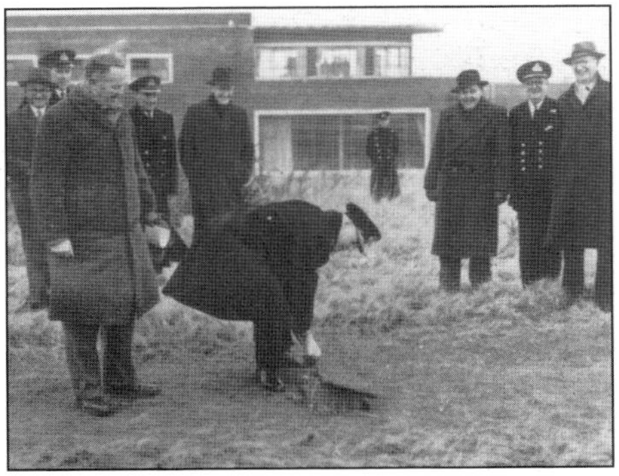

Although many of the smaller buildings had been completed, it wasn't until February 1952 that the construction of the main block was started. Admiral Sir John Edelston, then Commander-in-Chief, Portsmouth, is pictured cutting the first sod using a silver spade made especially by the workshops on the site.

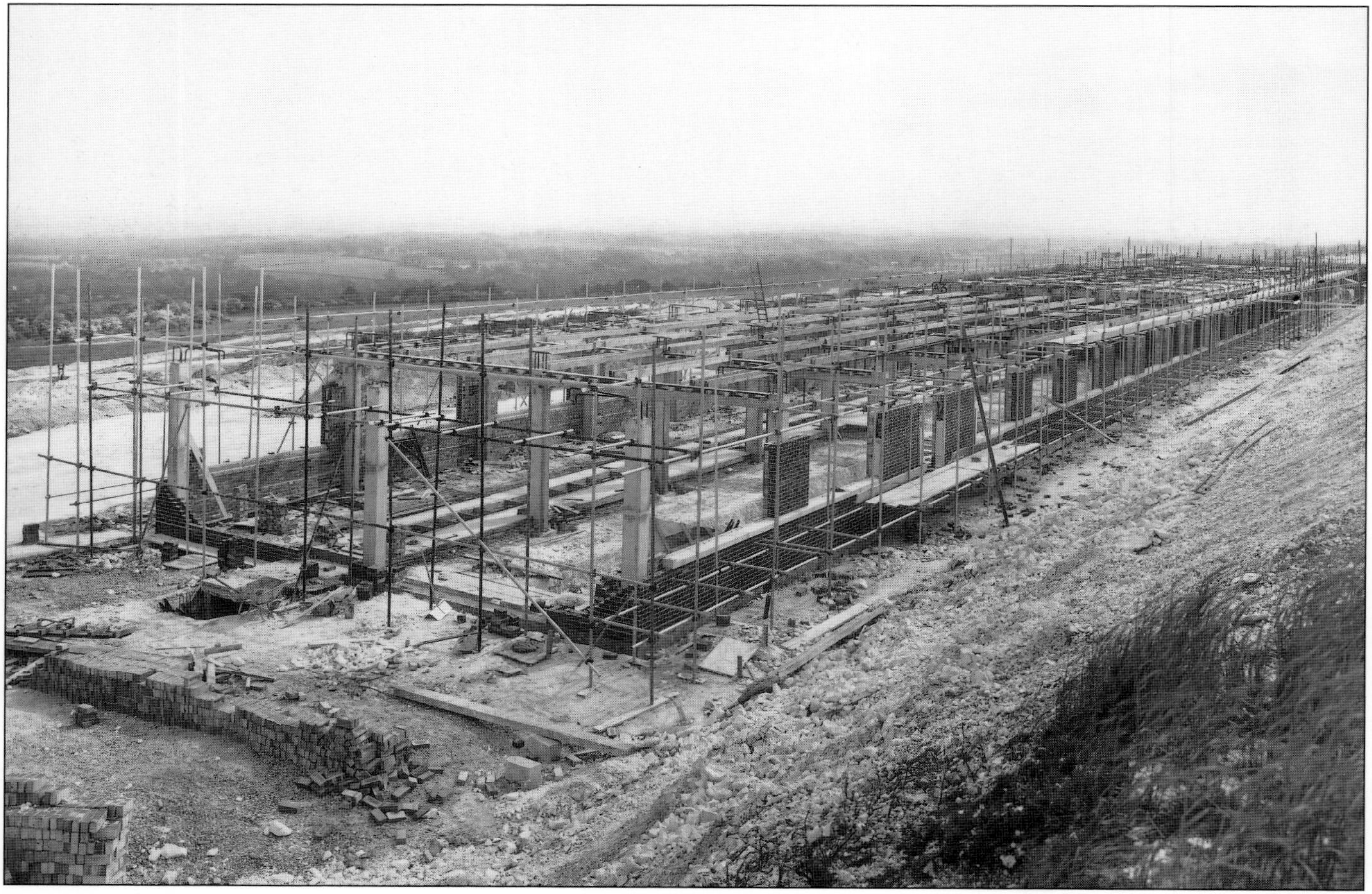

A maze of scaffolding and brickwork stretches out along the hilltop as the Ministry of Defence site construction continues.

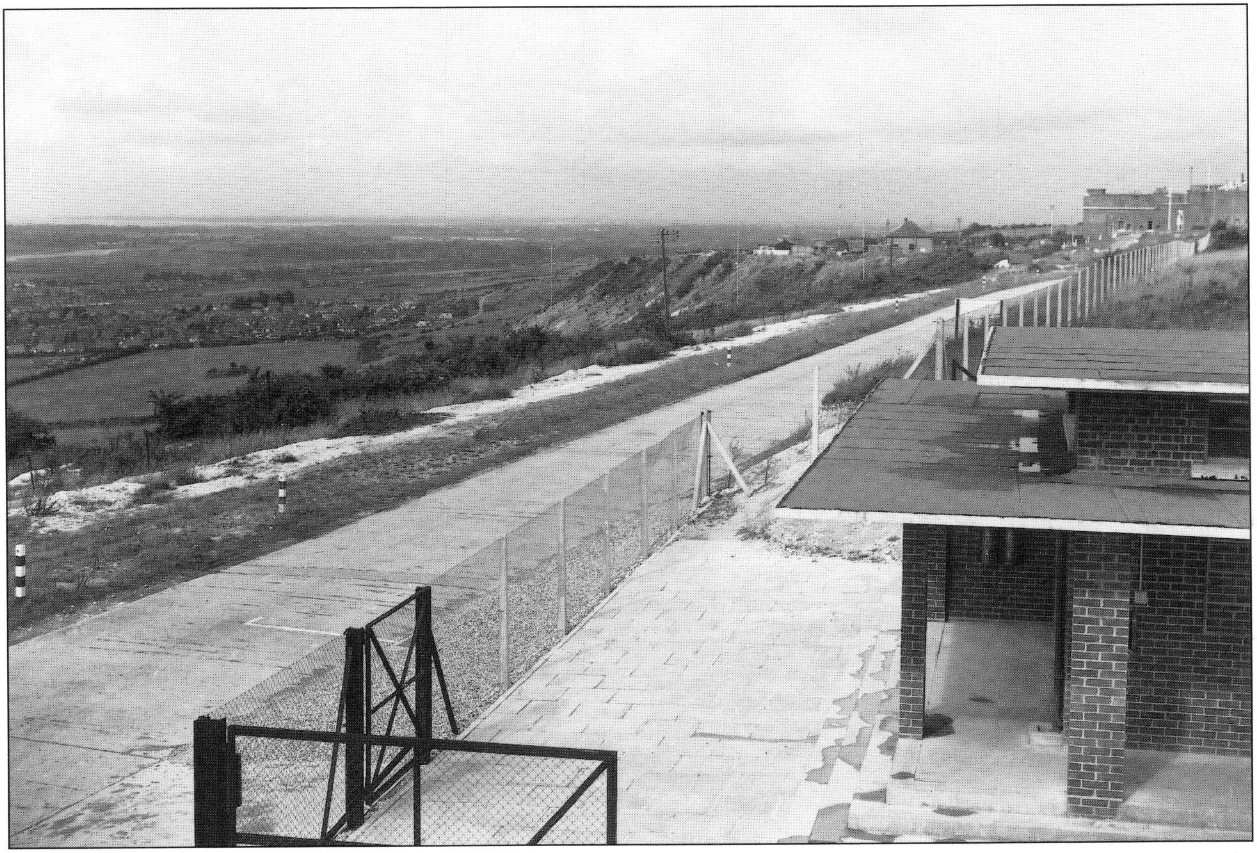

This 1950's photographer at the front gate of the complex has turned his camera towards the west bringing Fort Southwick into the picture.

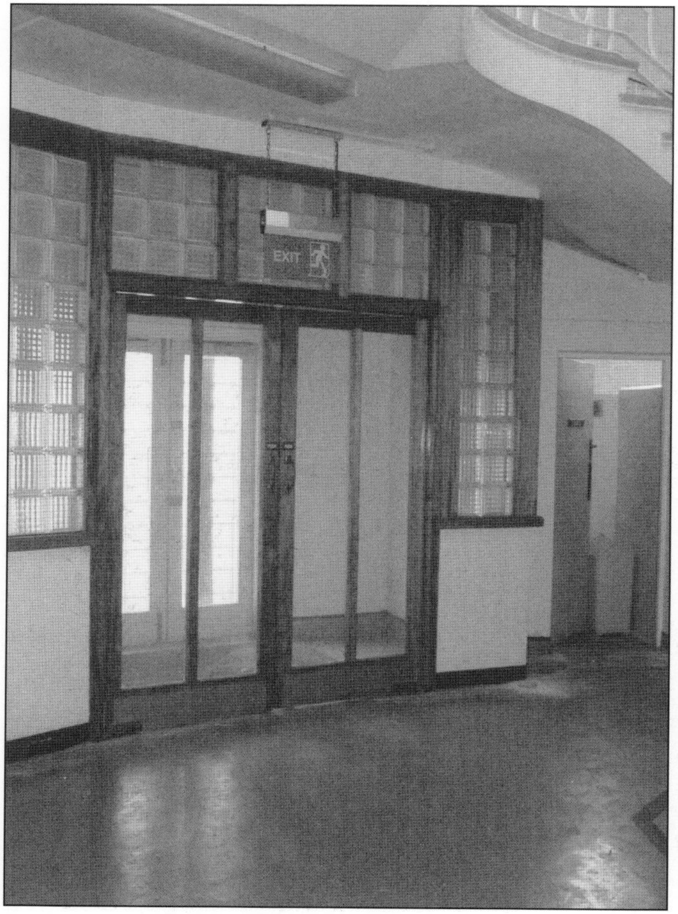

Even today, with Portsdown Main empty and awaiting a buyer, the interior still retains its art deco elegance.

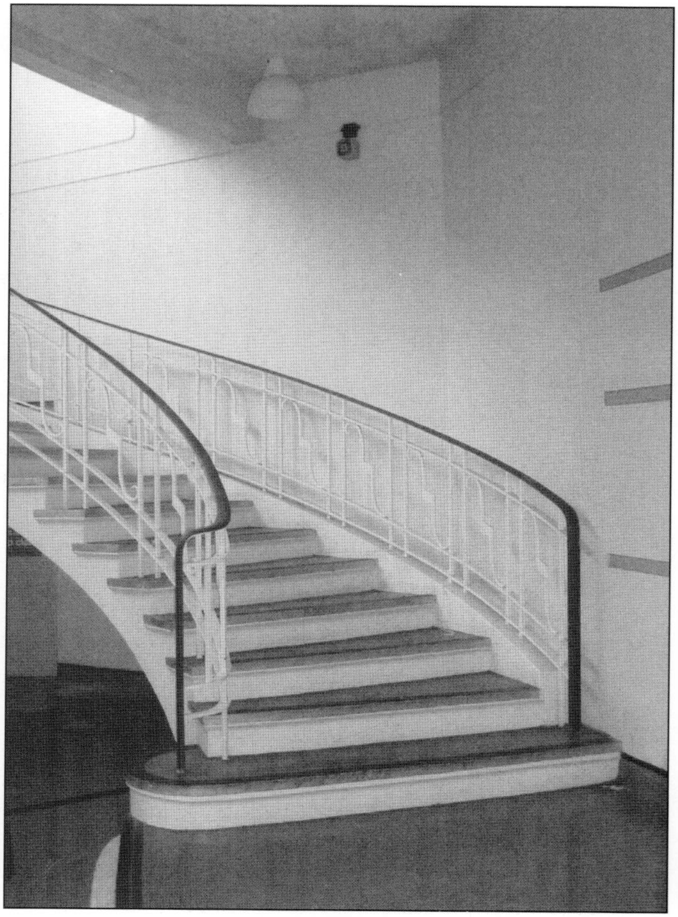

The curving stairs and wrought iron balustrade must have once hummed with workers using the building.

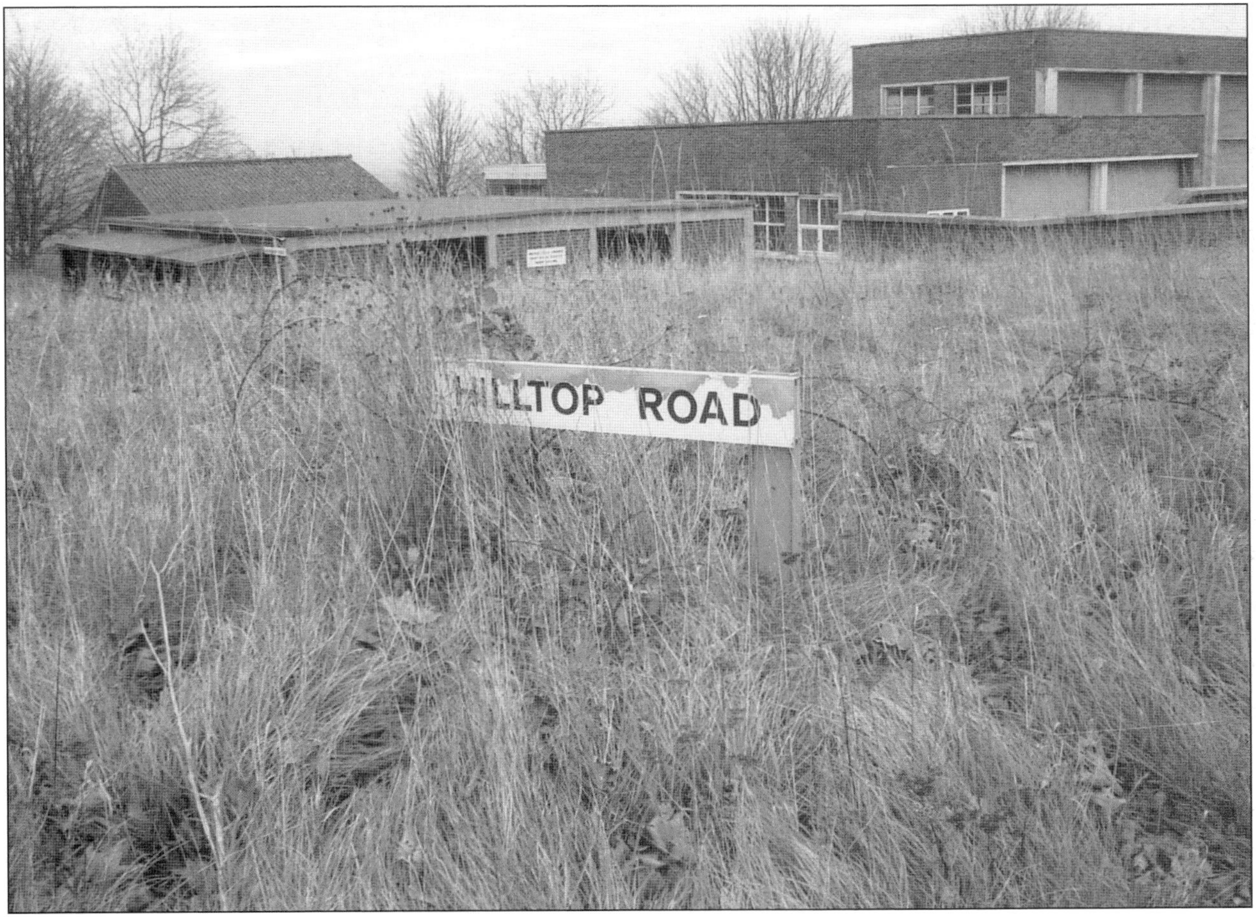

A simple road sign, within the complex, leaves no doubt as to the position of the Ministry of Defence site.

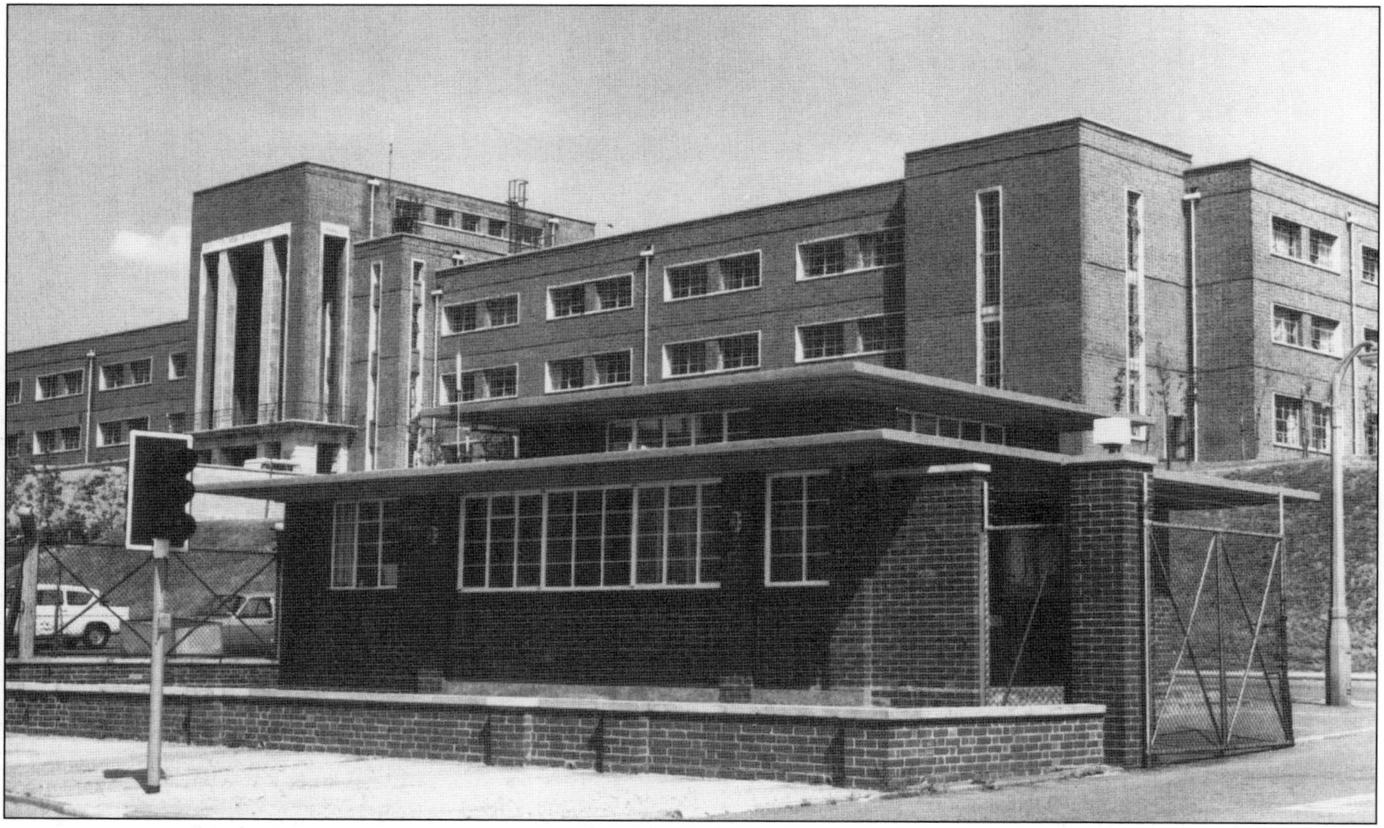

The final picture in this section depicts Portsdown Main as most people remember it, although this shot was taken in 1960 at the time that the site had its own set of traffic lights.

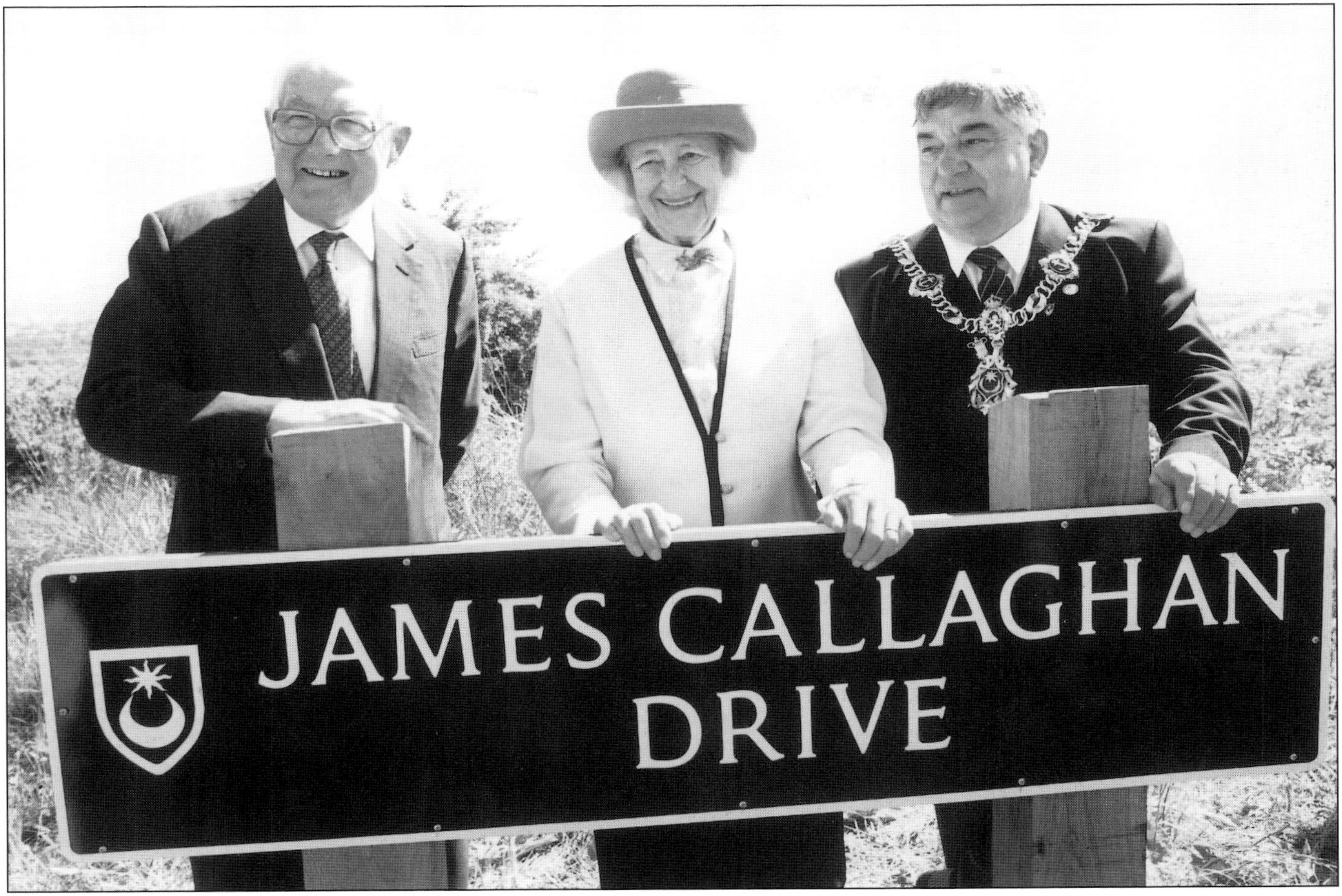

When the Ministry of Defence decided it had no more use for the military road that ran along the top of the hill, it was decided to honour a famous son of Portsmouth. In May 1997 former Prime Minister James Callaghan returned to the city of his birth – and in keeping with his soubriquet of Sunny Jim he brought a bright day with him – to declare open James Callaghan Drive. Lord Callaghan is pictured with his wife Lady Audrey Callaghan and the then Lord Mayor of Portsmouth, Councillor Tony Golds. Lord Callaghan, who was made a Freeman of Portsmouth in 1991, died at his home in West Sussex in March 2005, on the eve of his 93rd birthday, but his name will always be remembered on Portsdown.

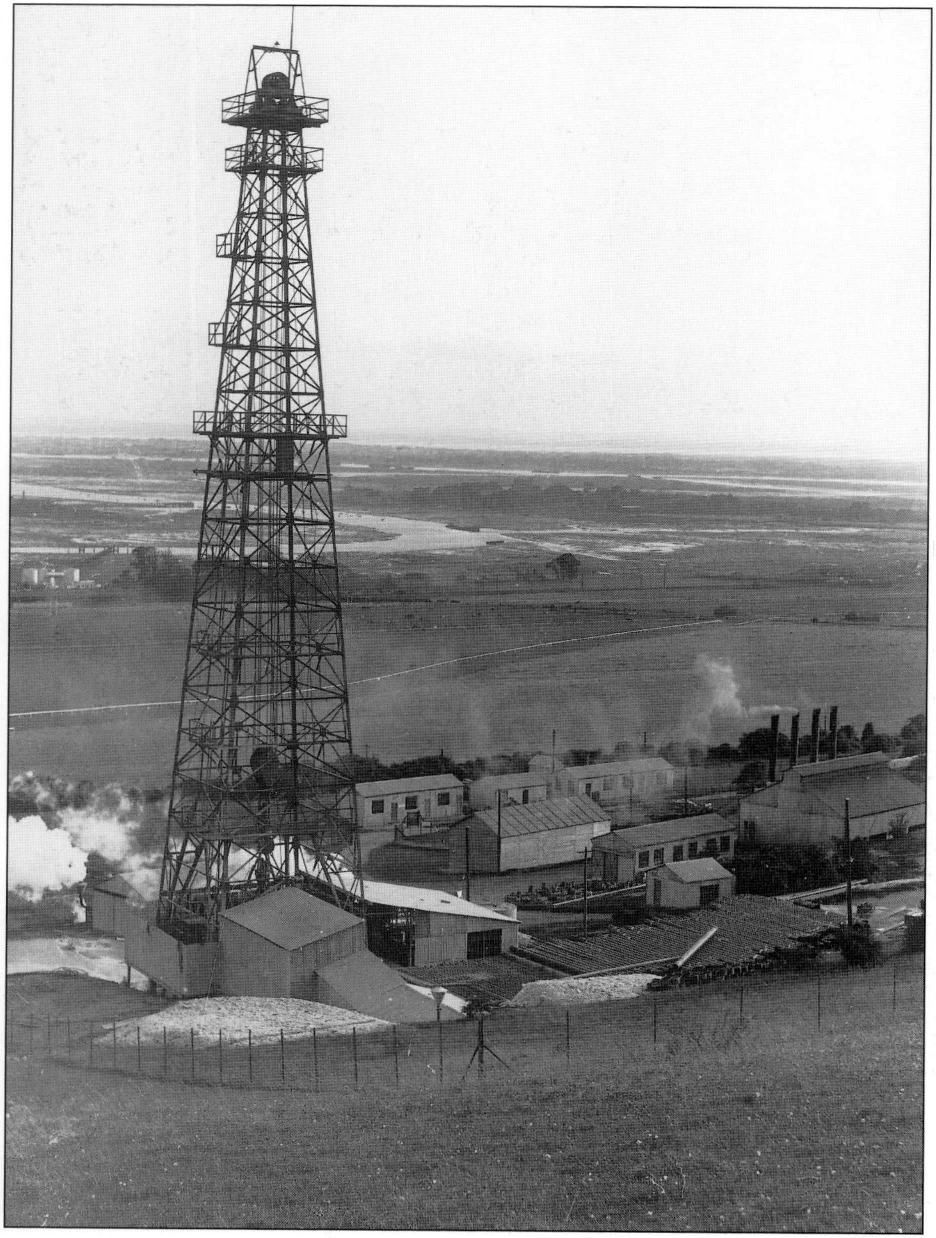

On 30 March 1936 the D'Arcy Exploration Company – part of Anglo-Iranian Oil – started what they claimed was the first seeking of oil in England, and all on the slopes of Portsdown Hill. The oil was to be pumped to the Paulsgrove quay, seen at the left of the picture, but in the event nothing was found and the project was relinquished on 17 February 1938. A small town grew up around the 130ft high drilling rig. Four boilers, each with a tall chimney, were constructed to generate the steam to drive the drills, each boiler being fed from a 1200-gallon water tank. The white perimeter fence of Wymering racecourse can be clearly seen in the background.

Portsmouth racecourse at Wymering catered for speedway races as well as the traditional meetings. It opened on 10 August, 1928, and was considered to be one of the best courses in the country, and was turfed with 40,000 square yards of grass cut from the face of Portsdown Hill.

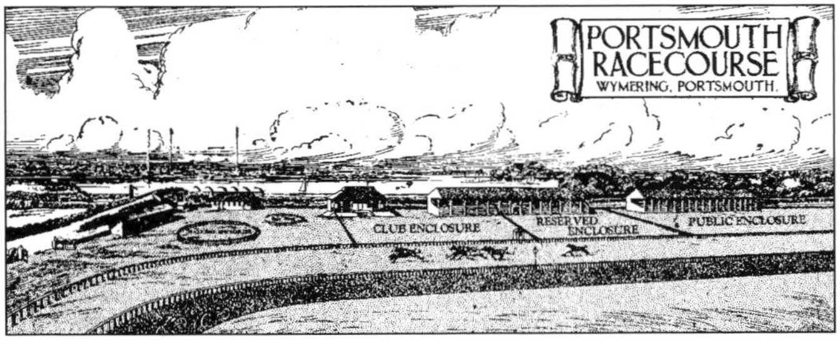

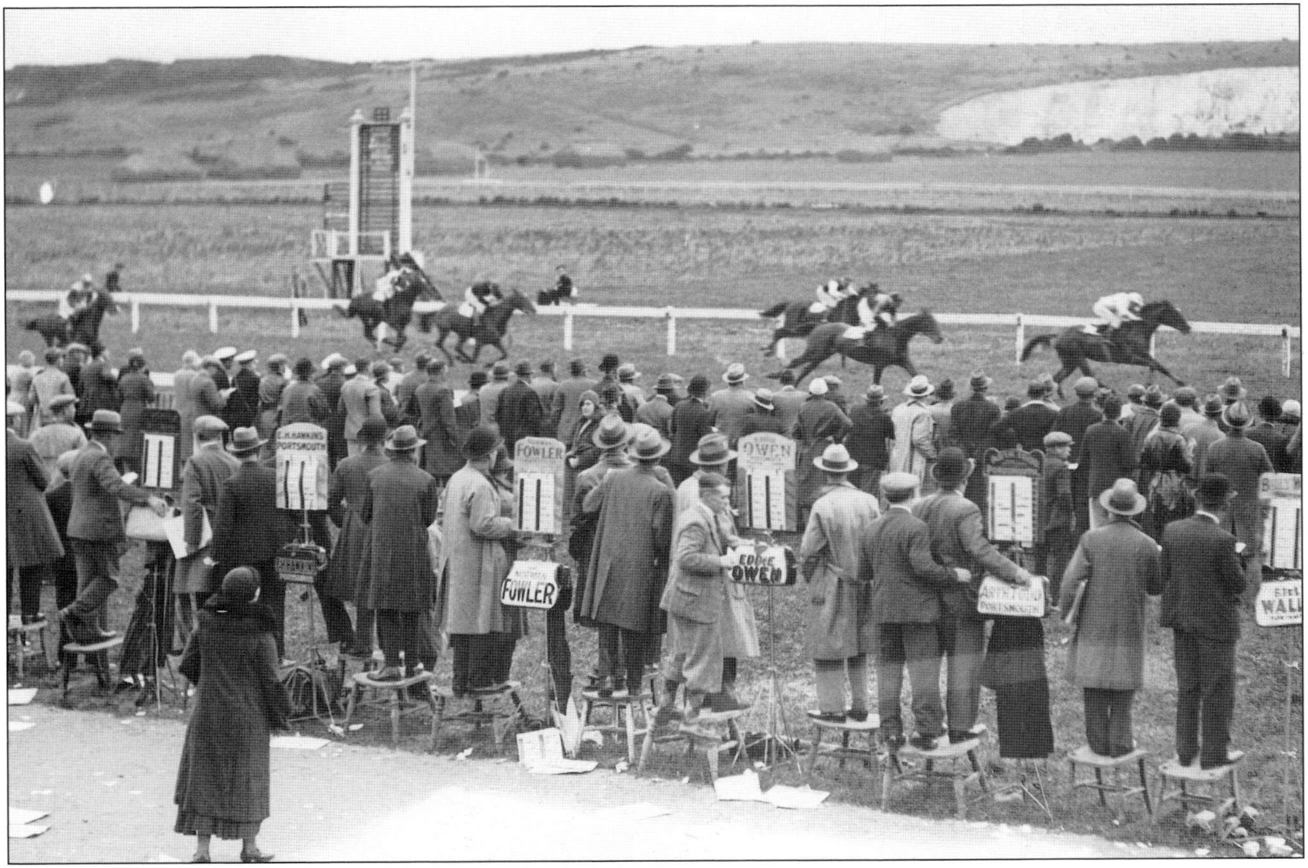

Backed by the chalk pits on Portsdown Hill, bookmakers stand on their stools to get a good view of the race over the heads of punters at Portsmouth Racecourse.

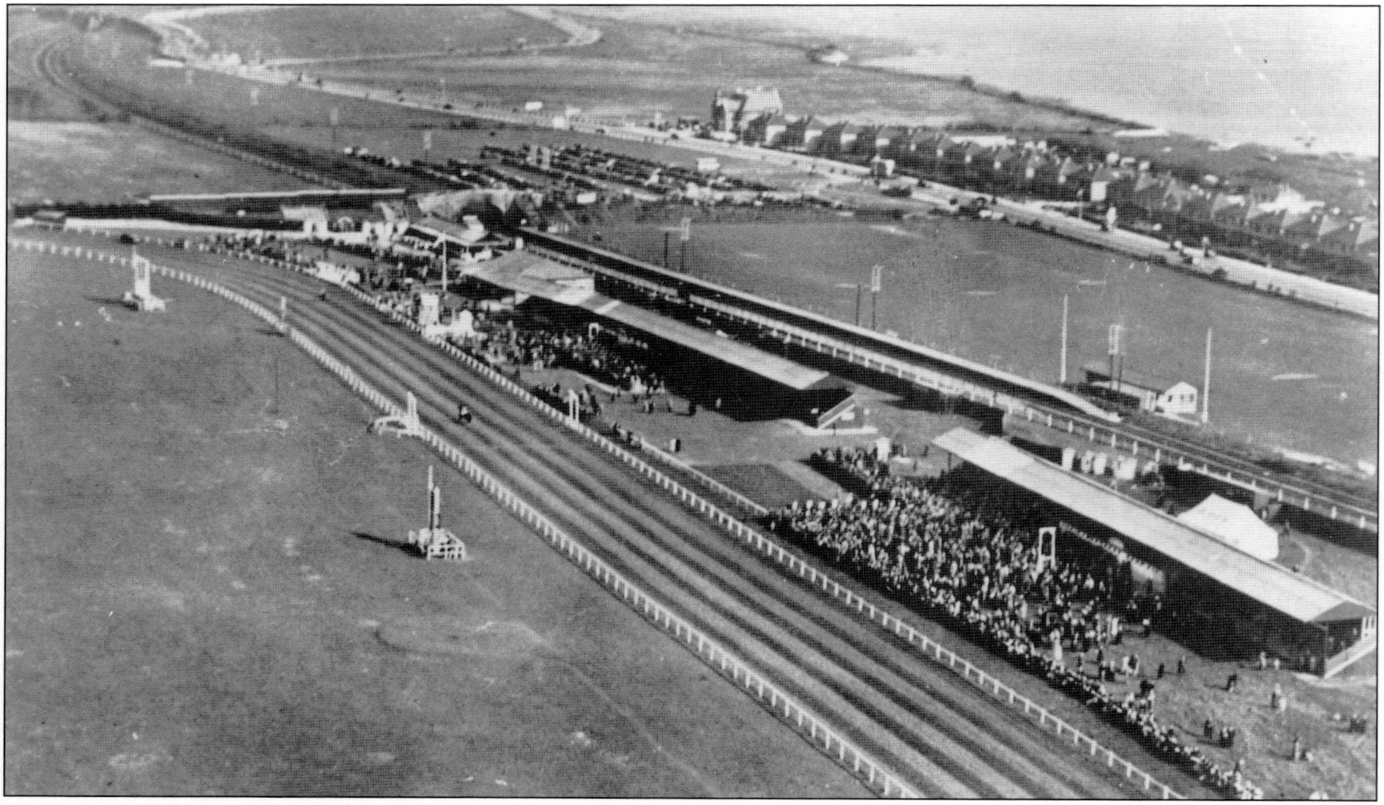

This picture of Wymering racecourse from the air shows the course, the stands, and in the background the tiny railway station that was built to accommodate race-goers. Racecourse Lane is the only reminder of the track which operated until the beginning of the war.

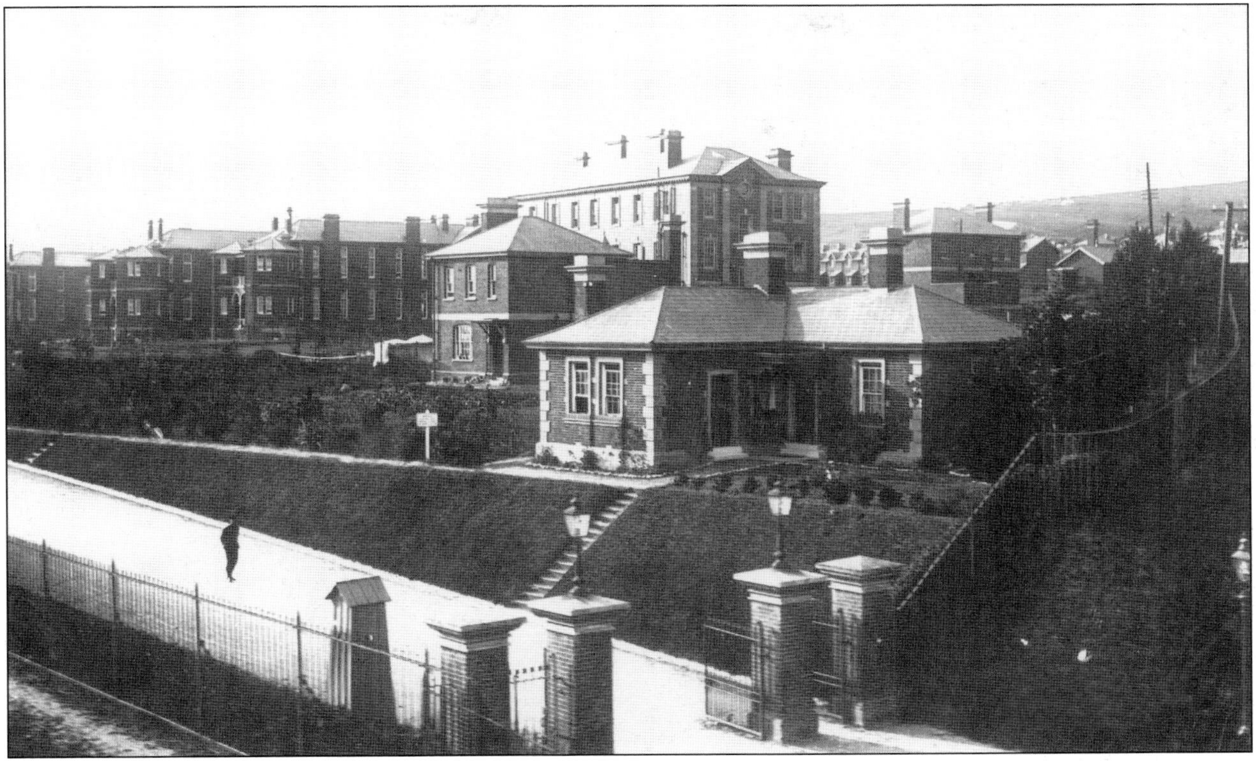

Queen Alexandra Hospital started life as the Alexandra military hospital. Building started in 1904 and the hospital was ready to receive patients by 1908. This picture shows the original complex and the main gate.

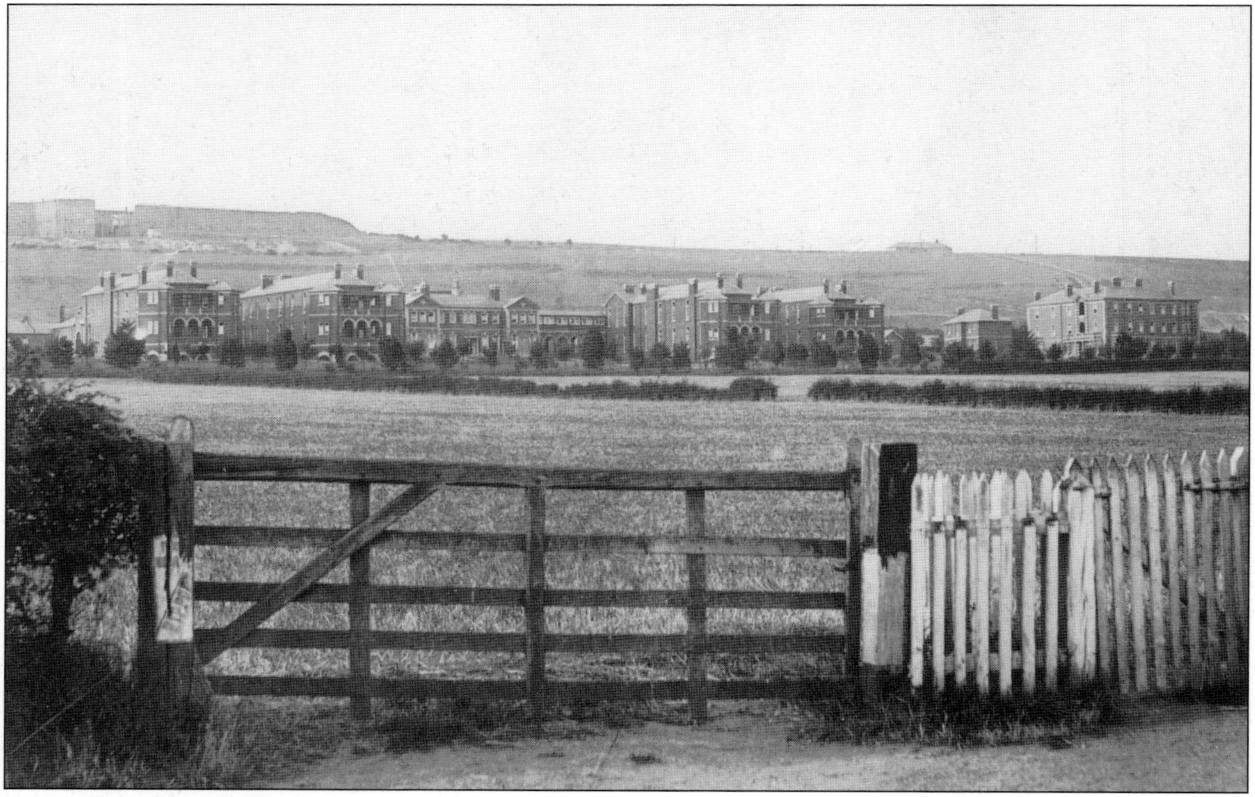

From the south Portsdown Hill still has a pastoral look, even with the brand-new hospital on the slopes. On the skyline can be seen Fort Widley and the roof of Fairhouse Cottage.

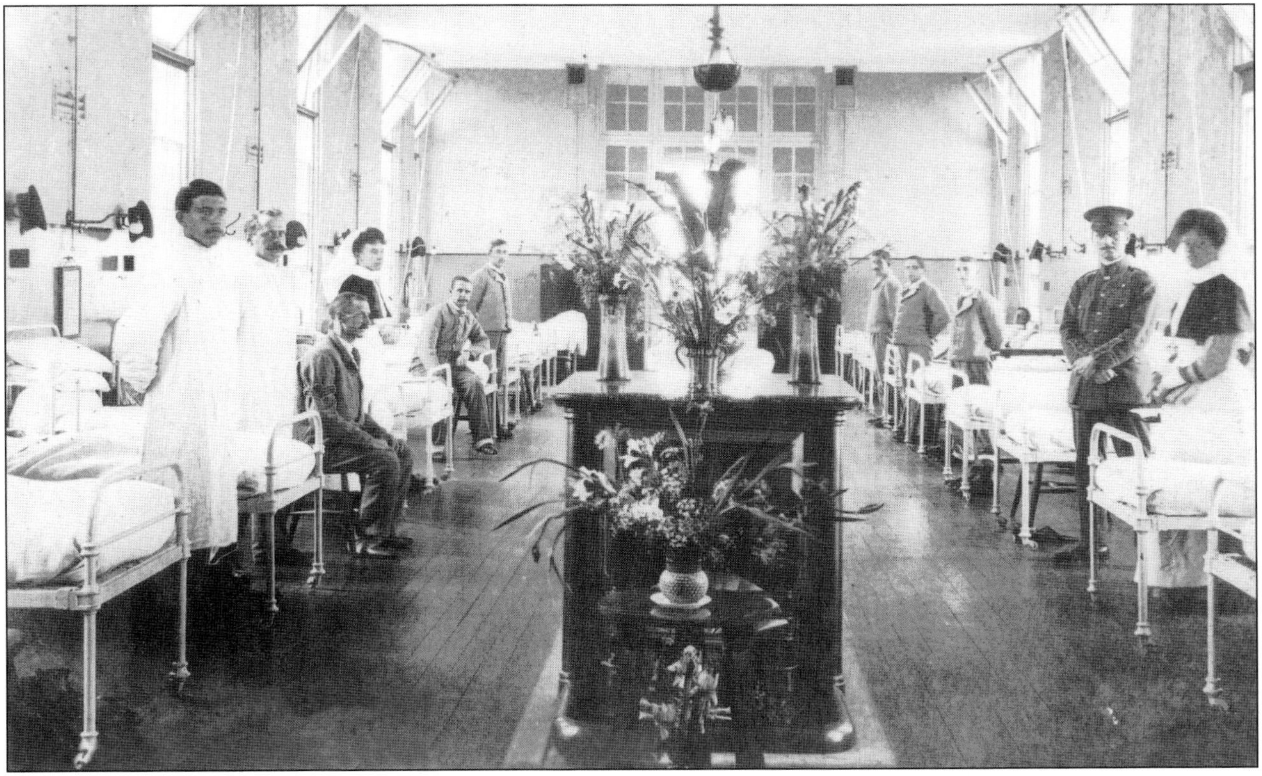

Above: *Patients and staff stand to attention for the photographer, with the exception of two patients who are obviously sitting to attention.*

Right: *All equipment that Edwardian surgery could provide is visible in the operating theatre at the Alexandra military hospital.*

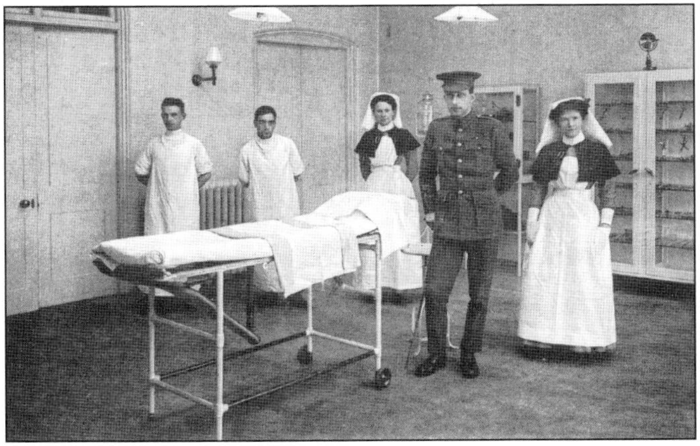

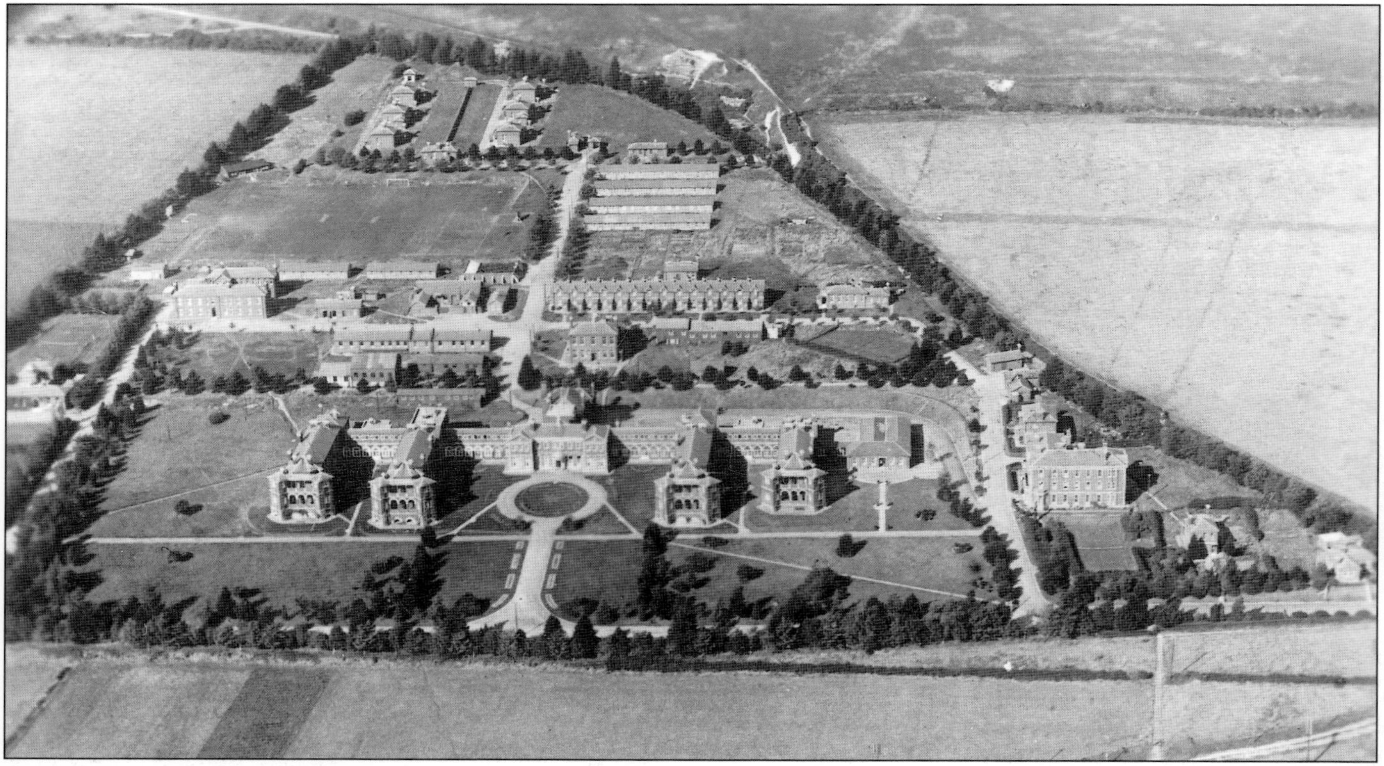

A cameraman from Surrey Flying Services flew over the hospital during the period of peace between the wars showing the 22-acre site. To the top of the picture are the extra buildings erected to cater for servicemen injured in the Great War.

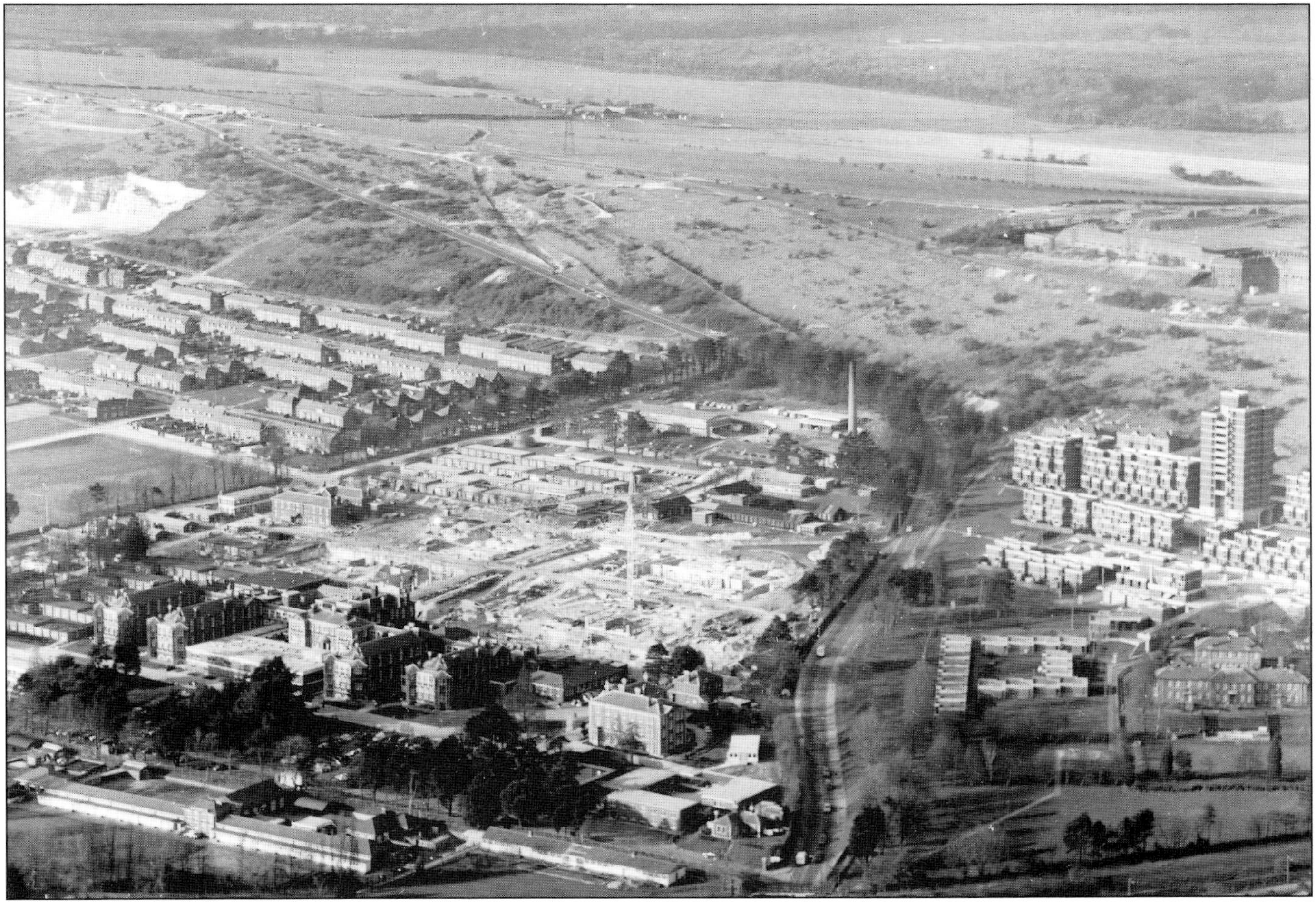

After the Second World War the hospital became a civilian unit, and in the '70s a whole new hospital was constructed around the original building. This superb aerial view shows the huge building site that the complex had become in the name of progress.

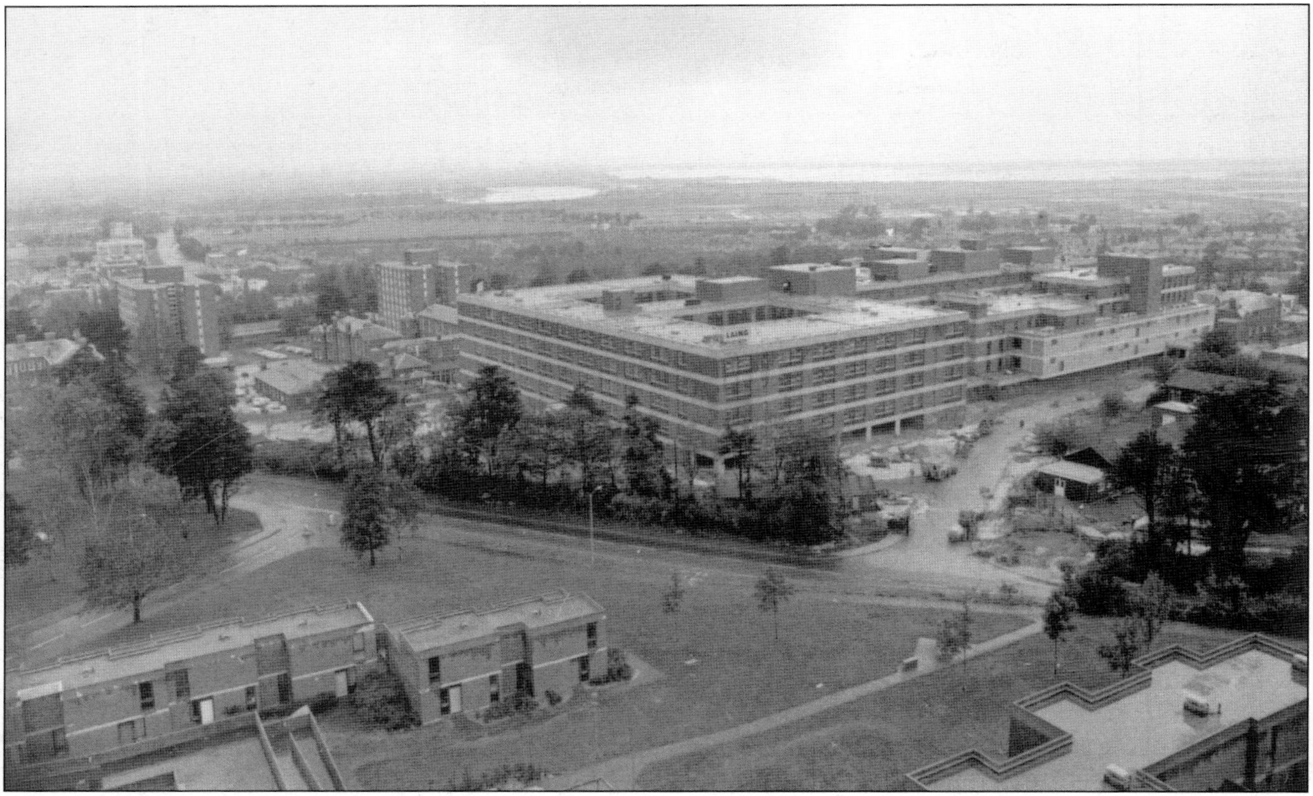

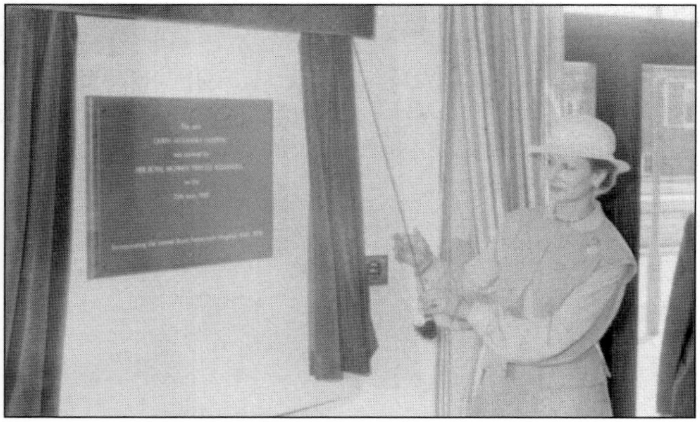

Above: *The photographer has taken to the heights of Portsdown Park to secure this view of QA with the construction crews still in occupation.*

Left: *On 25 June 1980, Princess Alexandra officially opened the new Queen Alexandra Hospital.*

Water has been stored at Farlington since 1811 when the Drayton Basin reservoir, seen in the centre of the picture, was built to supply Portsmouth with its daily drinking water. This is now the site of Solent Road Infant School. The present site of the treatment works was started in 1869 with the building of two reservoirs, which have now been demolished.

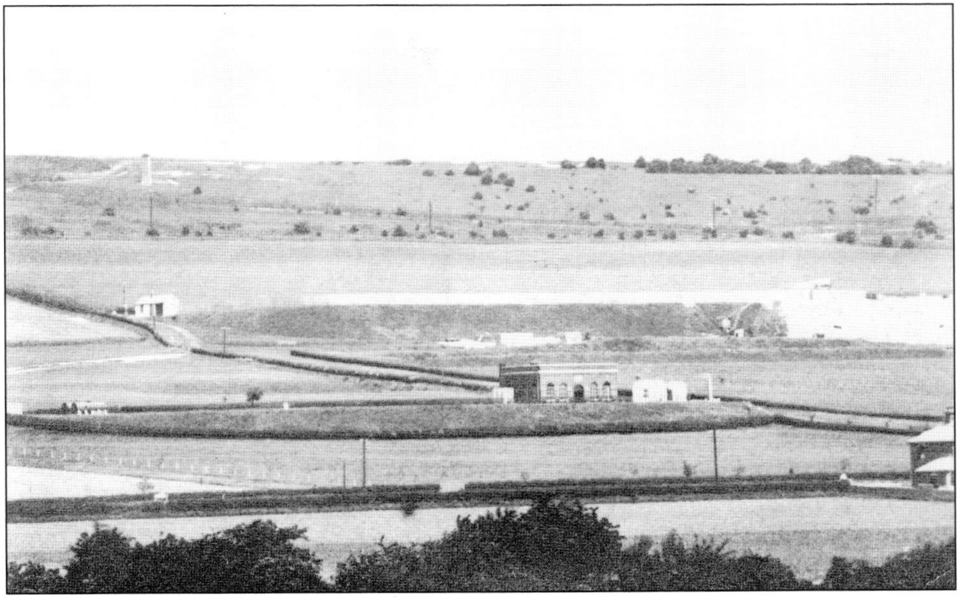

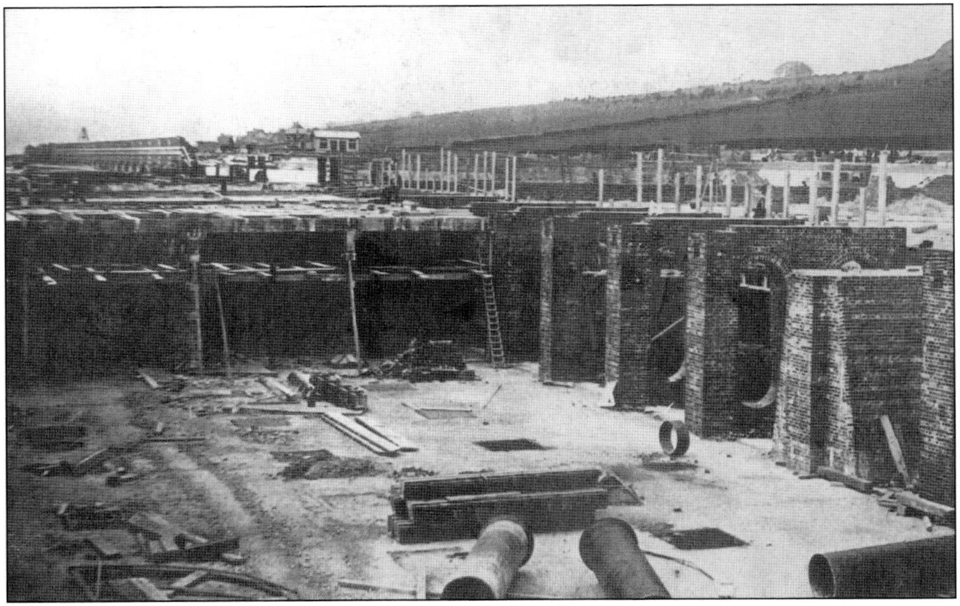

In 1909 two more reservoirs were built at the Farlington treatment works. Construction of the No 4 reservoir is seen here, destined to hold three million gallons when it came into operation in the following year.

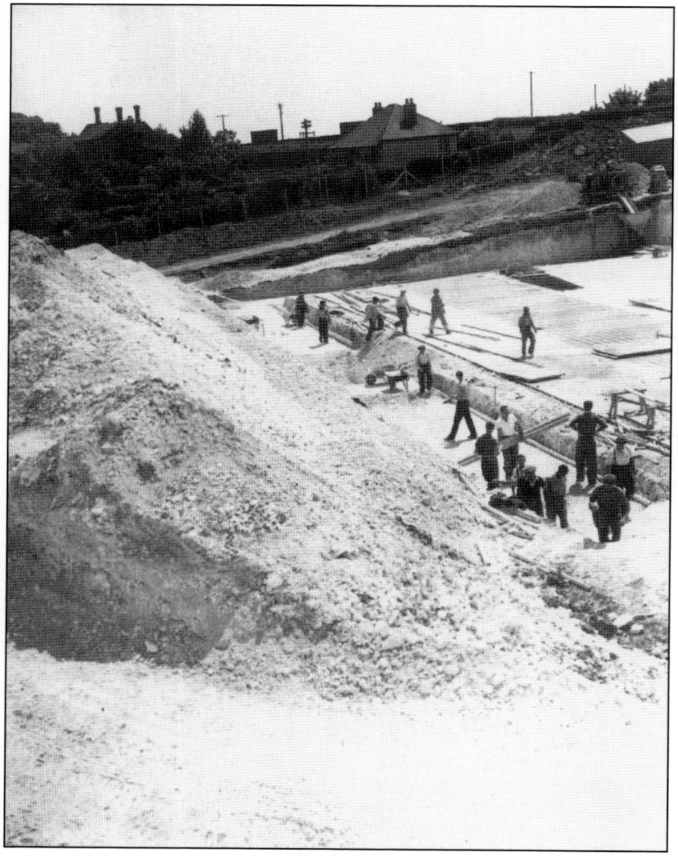

In the thirties a further underground reservoir was built near the George. The workforce is pictured here dwarfed by the huge mound of chalk spoil.

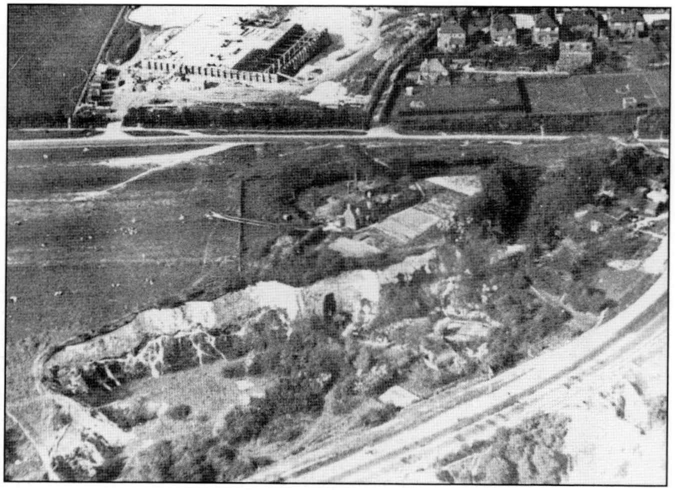

The George reservoir is clearly seen in this aerial view. The London Road is snaking northwards at the bottom of the picture, with the chalk cutting now occupied by Cliffdale Gardens in the centre of the view.

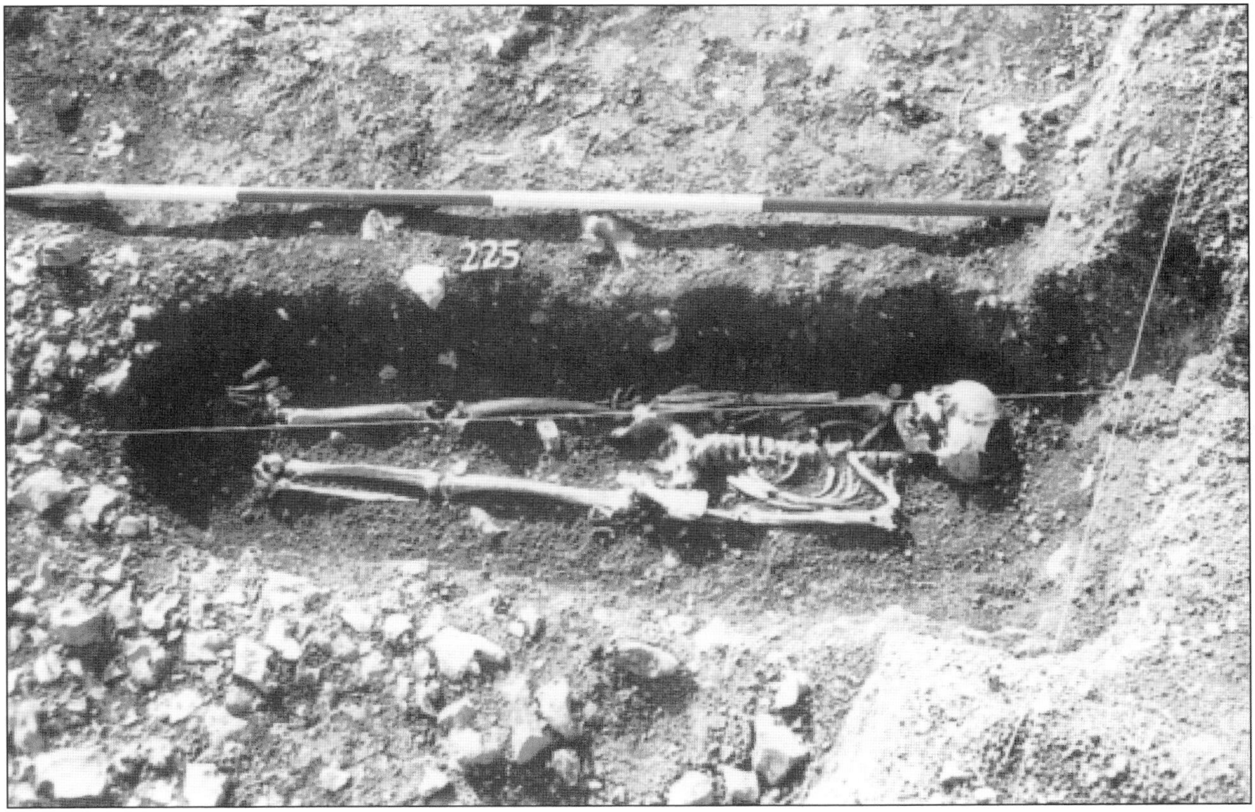

Portsdown was home to early man who left behind burial sites or barrows, topped in many cases by distinctive mounds. Between 1974 and 1976 a team of archaeologists excavated the Neolithic long barrow known as Bevis's Grave at Camp Down, with help from Havant College students. This picture shows one of the Saxon skeletons found during the excavations.

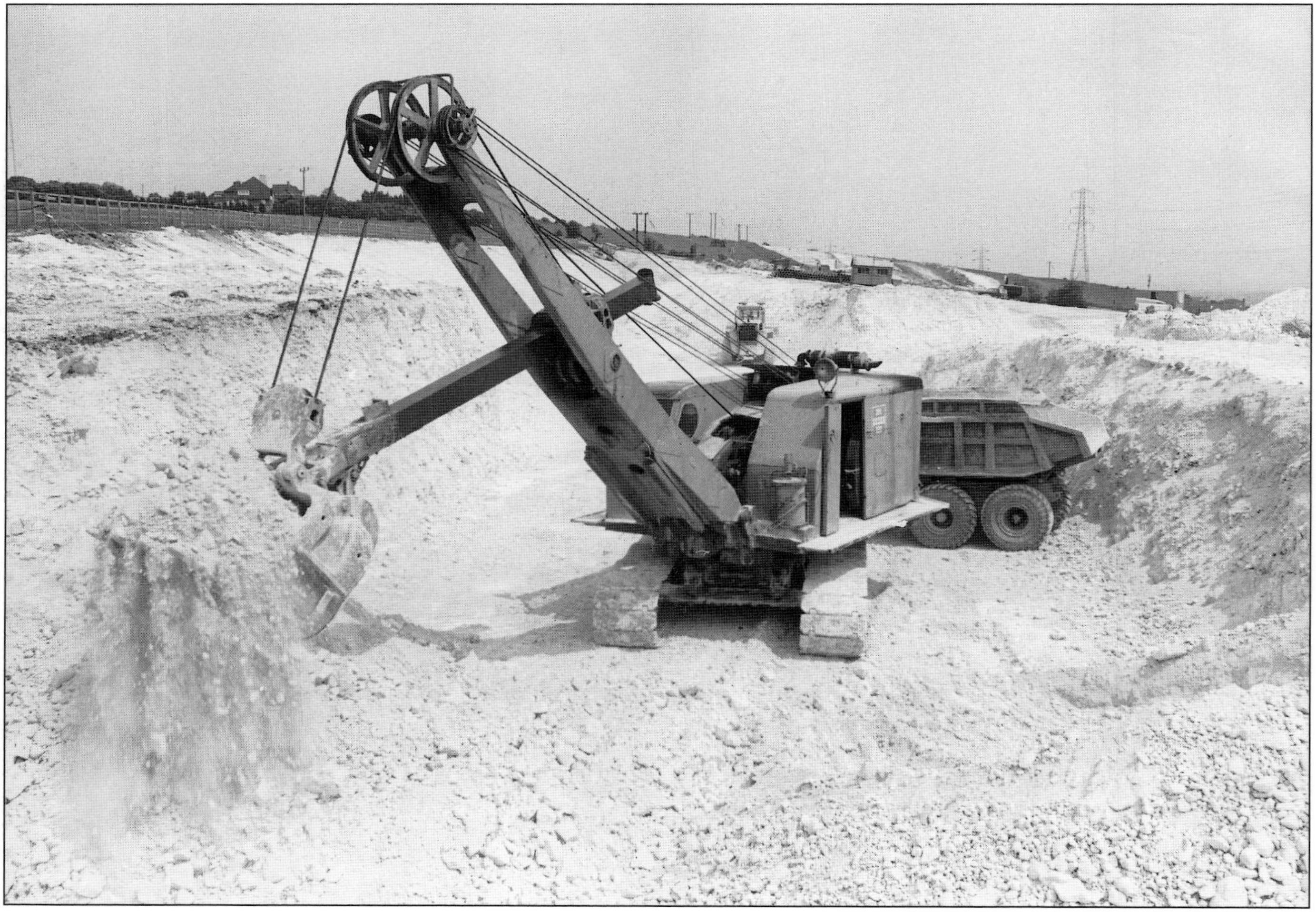

The year is 1971 and Portsdown Hill assumes a lunar landscape look as the heavy machinery removes tons of chalk for the M27 cutting.

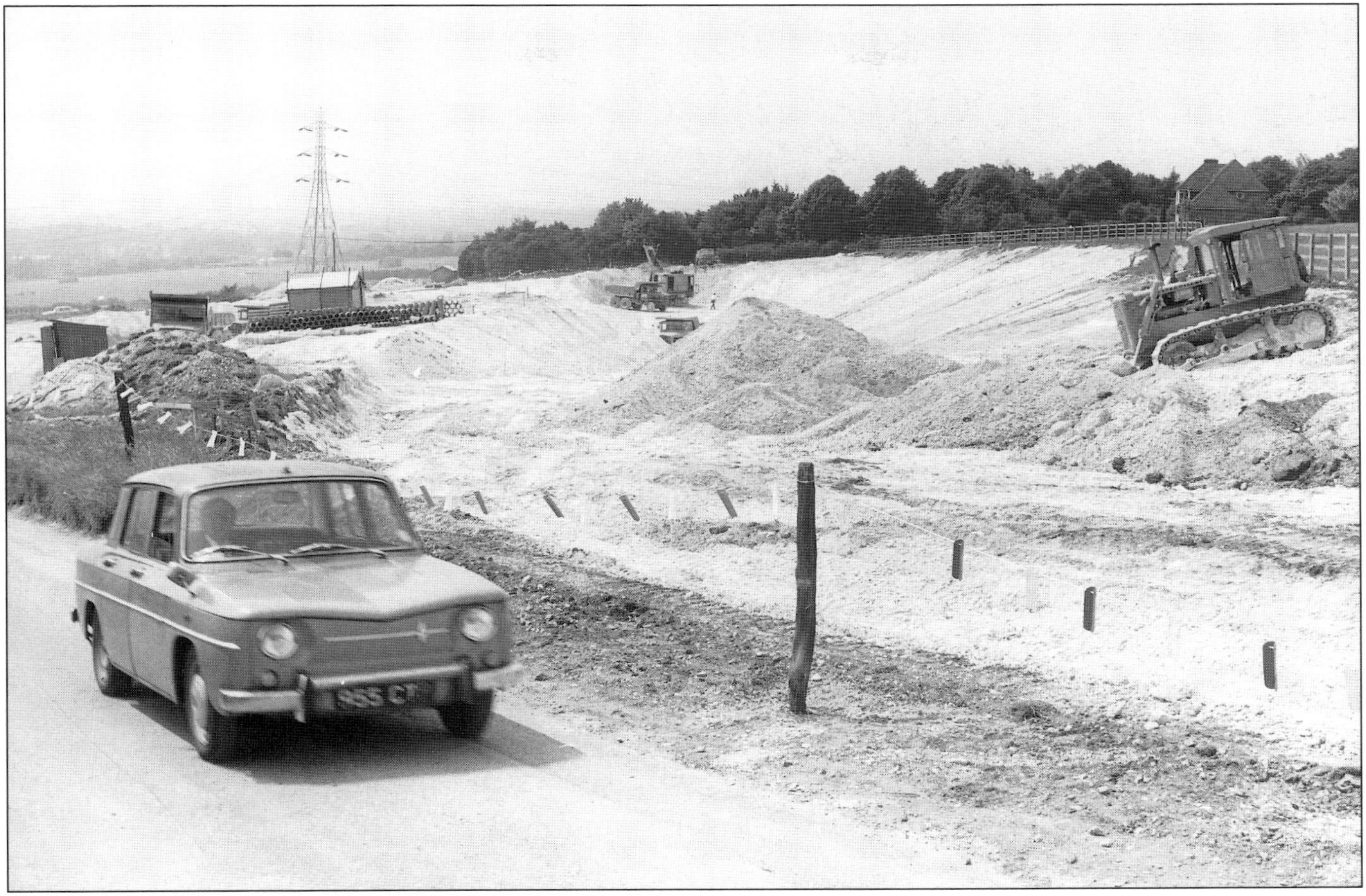

Skew Road, north of the village of Portchester, is a sea of chalk and building materials as the work progresses.

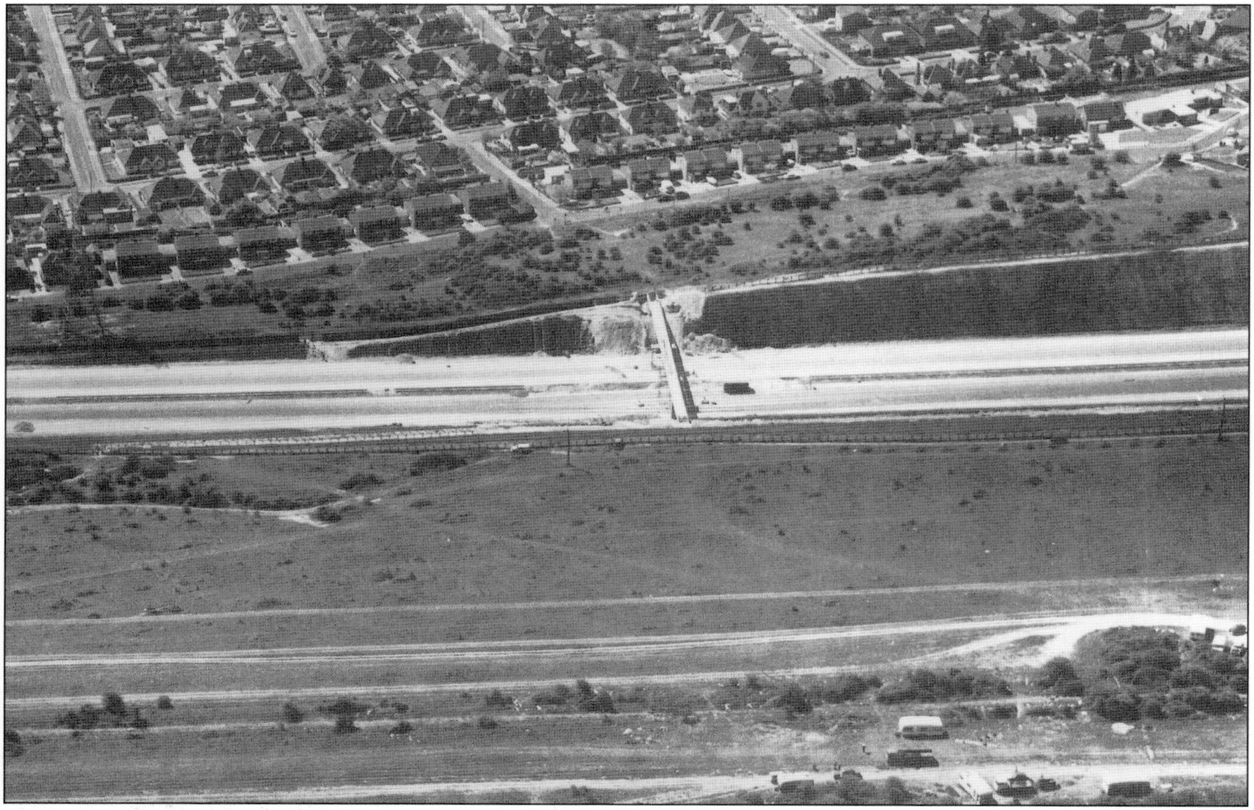

The motorway is well on target by May 1972 with work being undertaken on the footbridge north of Portchester. Portsdown Hill Road is at the bottom of the picture with Portchester spread out above.

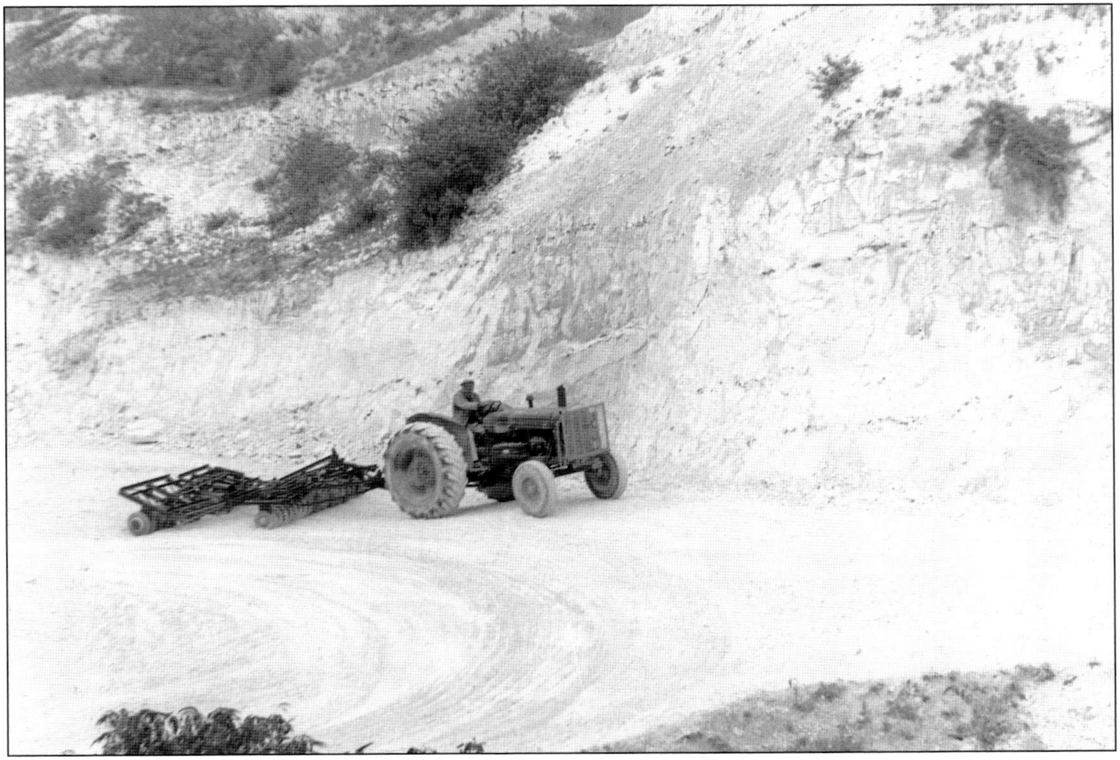

Above: *Later, when the M275 was built, much of the chalk needed for the construction came from the last working chalk pit on Portsdown Hill, situated off Hill Road, Portchester. Here a worker rakes the chalk before it is loaded on to trucks for the journey to the motorway site. Hill Road was originally called Abbott's Walk and formed the ancient track to Southwick Priory, which was used by the monks from Portchester Castle.*

Right: *By the '90s the pit had ceased working and some of the machinery was just left among the high white ridges where the chalk had been removed. Later the site was cleared and a small housing estate, Portchester Heights, now occupies the redundant pit.*

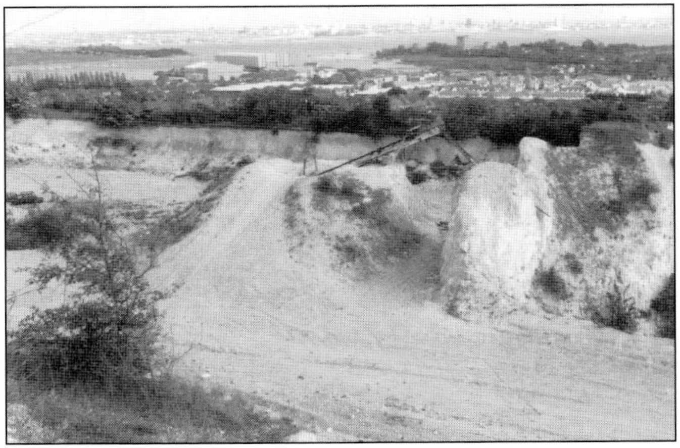

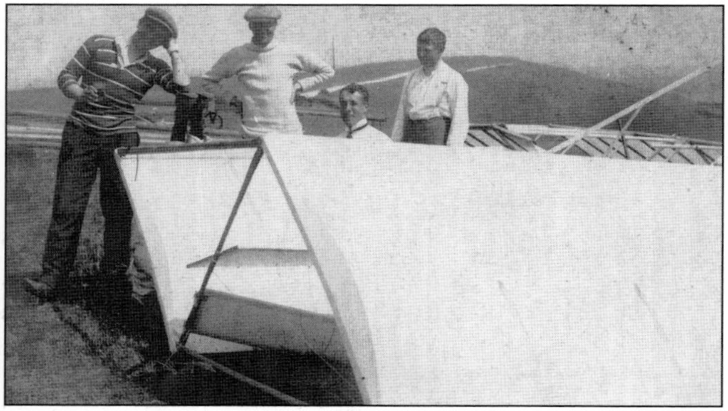

The Portsdown Hill slopes lent themselves to early gliding experiments. In August 1909 Southsea photographer and postcard publisher Stephen Cribb took this picture of a naval team – with one member standing on his head – taking a camera call during trials on the slopes. The two-man biplane glider was constructed at Fort Blockhouse, Gosport, and had been brought to the hill slopes on a trolley. The craft was launched from a set of wooden rails laid down the slope. Lieuts Porte and Pirie took their seats but as the glider took to the air its tailplane assembly struck the rails, bringing craft and crew down to earth. Although the glider was badly damaged no one was hurt and the two young officers went away to replan their airborne attempt.

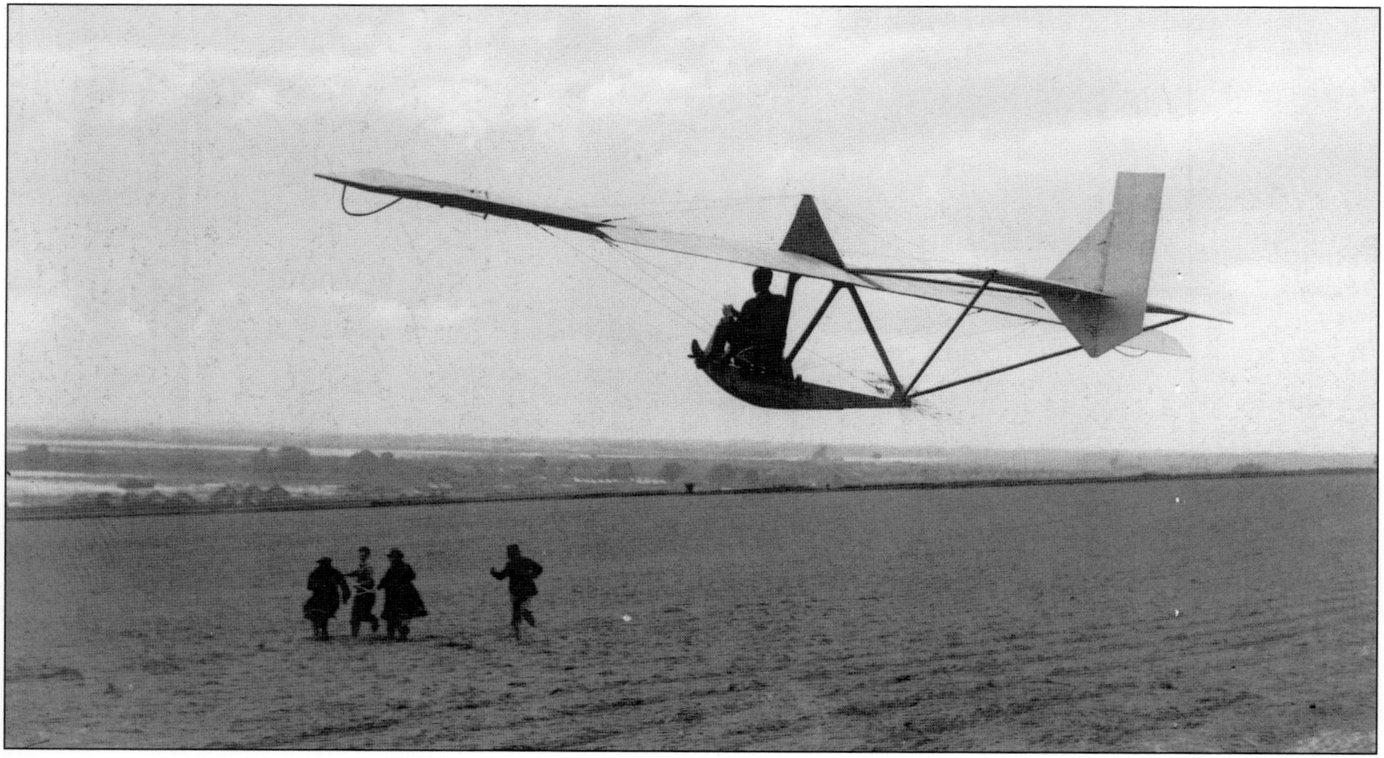

Later, in the '20s and '30s Portsmouth Gliding Club took to the slopes to seek thermals. Some machines were launched by being towed by a car, while others – like this Daglin trainer – took to the air with help from a few men and a long rope.

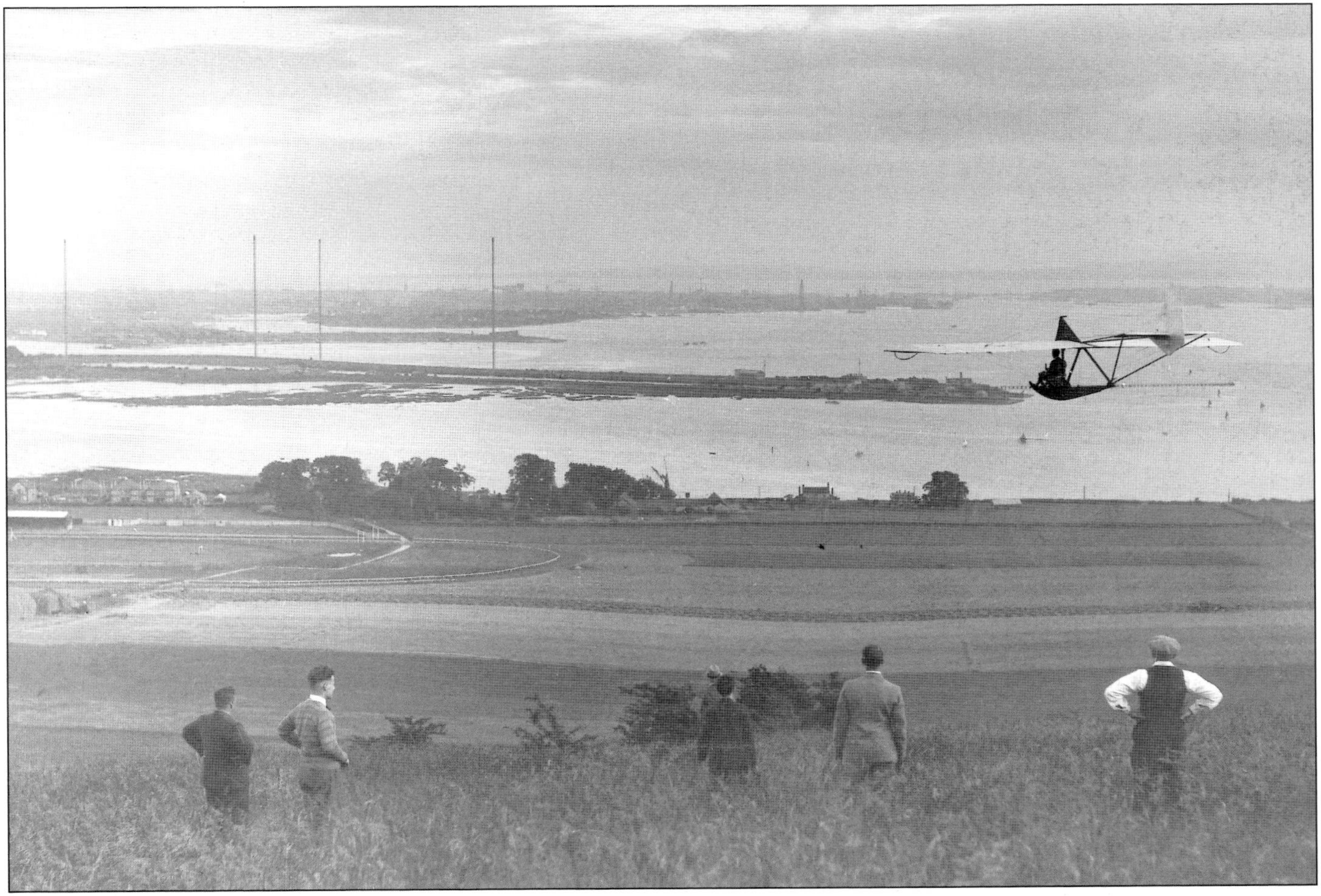

This moody shot shows the same machine in the air over the hill slopes. Again, in the middle background is the racecourse with the long white stand roof showing up clearly, while in the far background are the tall wooden aerials of Horsea Island.

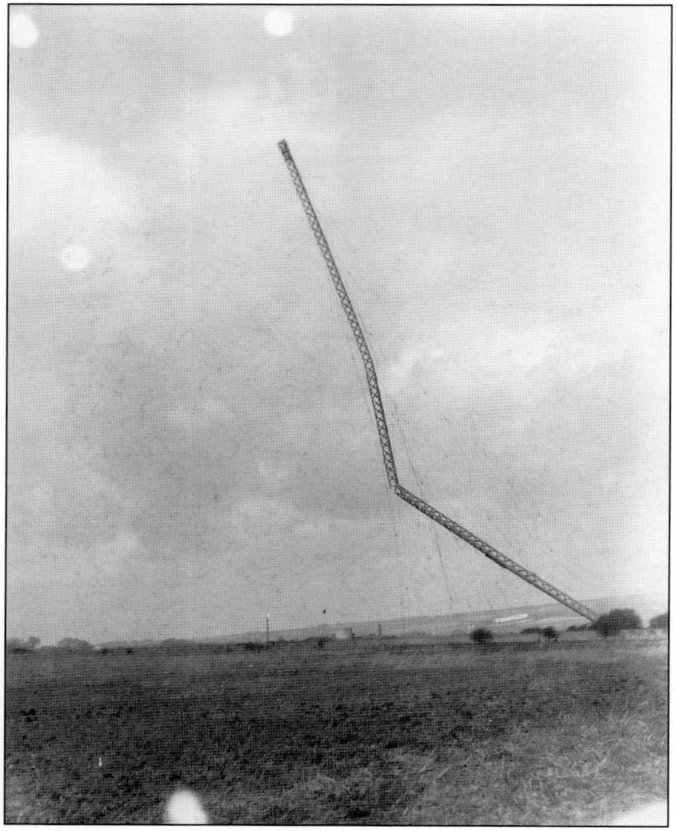

The Horsea aerials finally were brought to earth in the '30s. This evocative picture shows one of the huge wooden structures snapping as it is pulled down.

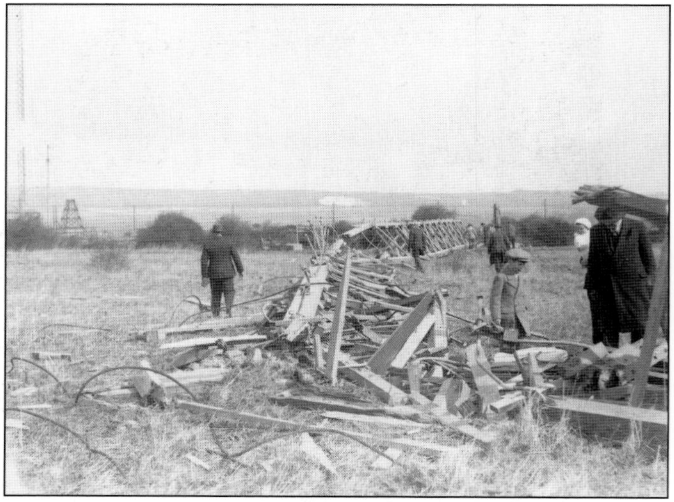

One of the huge aerials lies like a wounded giant on the grass at Horsea Island, generating interest from both young and old.

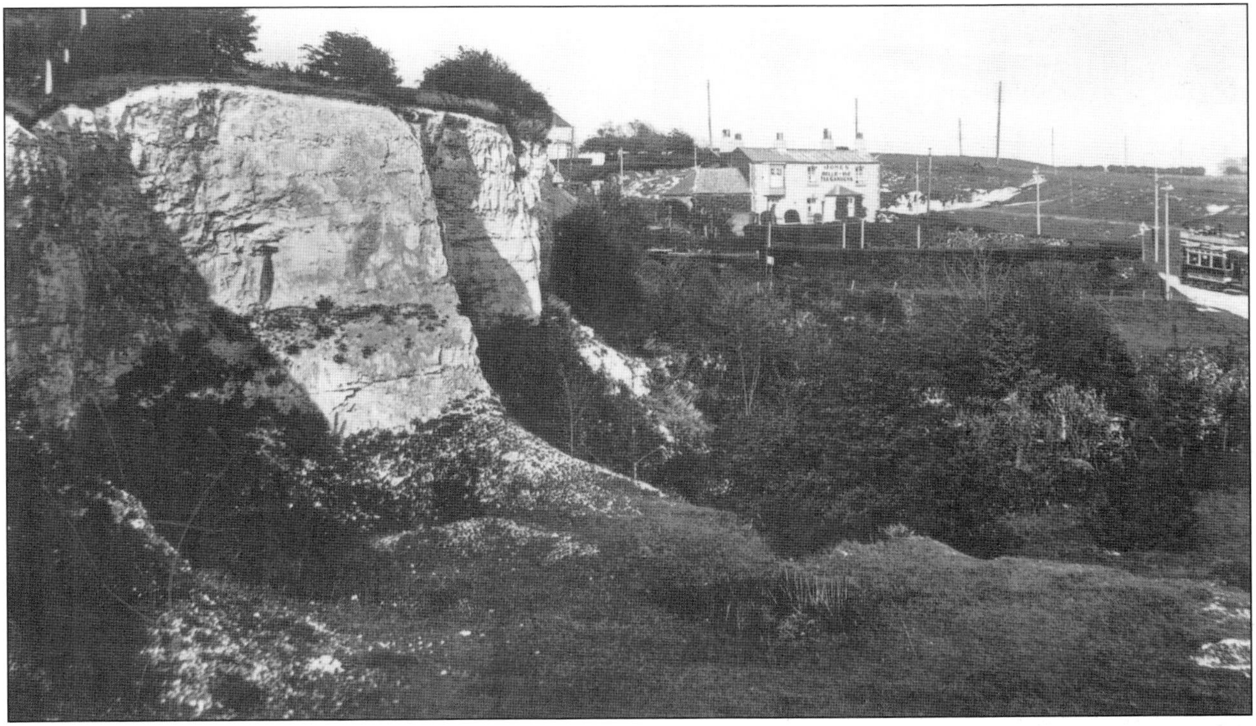

The tea gardens and a tram make a reappearance in the background in this postcard view of the cliffs, Portsdown. Candy's Pit is between the two high ridges. This part of the hill can be walked on the Candy's Pit Trail.

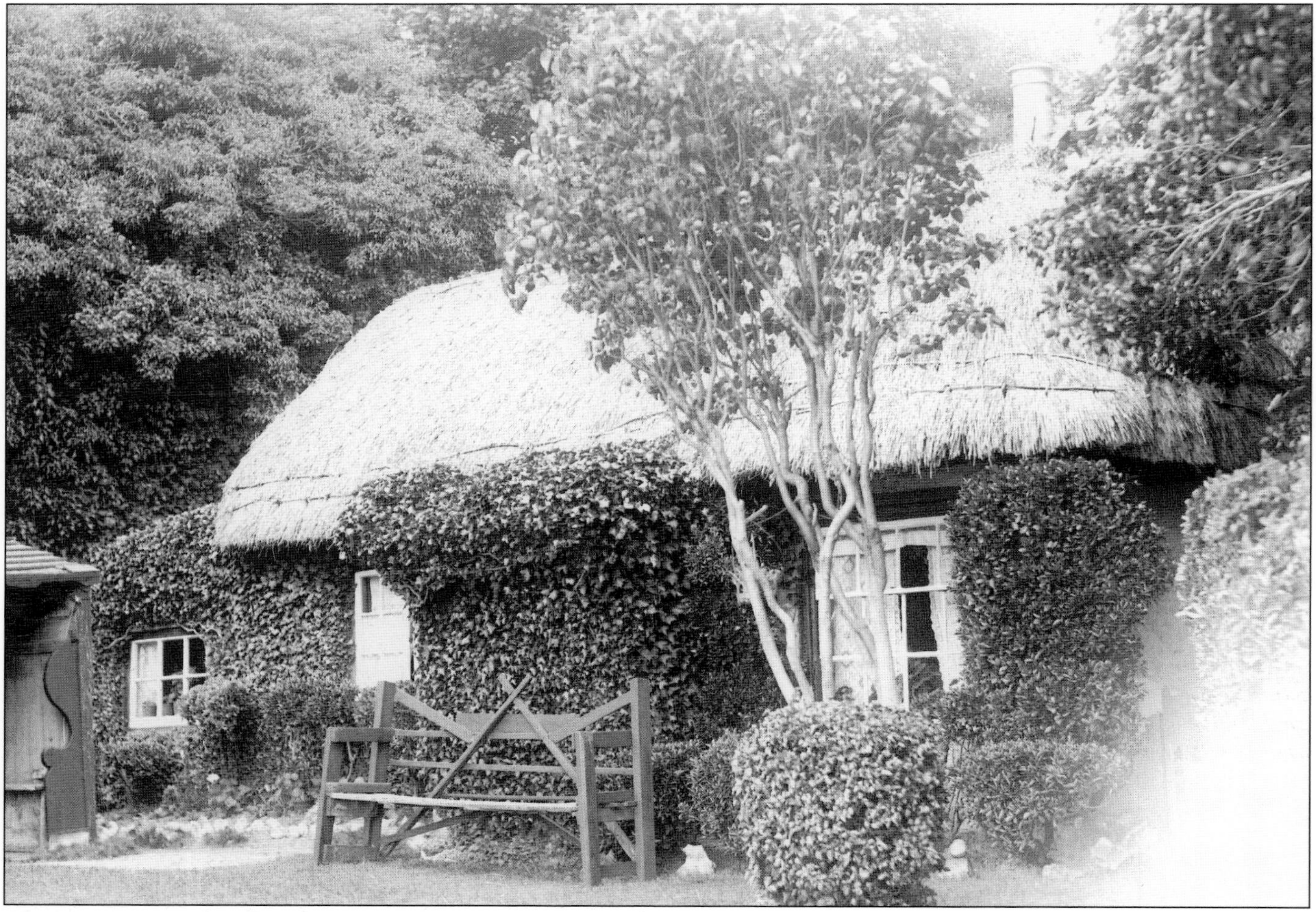

The old thatched cottage in Bell Pitt was a charming and popular place to stop as the owners operated it as tearooms.

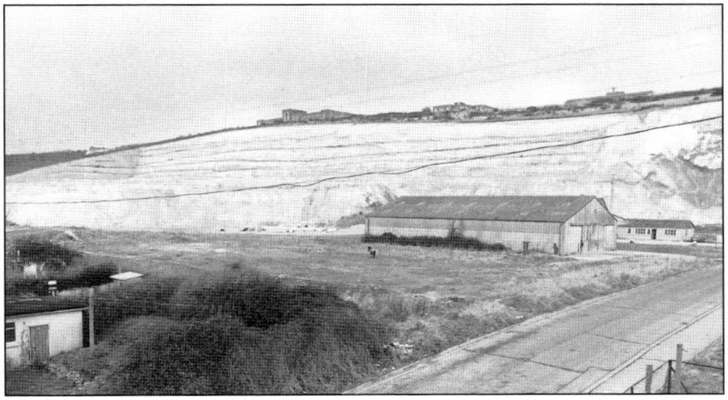

The cameraman has secured this image of Paulsgrove chalk pit on a cold January day in 1981. Portsdown Main dominates the hill skyline with a lot less construction than can be seen today.

Sir Arthur Conan Doyle never forgot Portsmouth after success and fame encouraged him to move away. In 'The Five Orange Pips', a story in The Adventures of Sherlock Holmes, *John Openshaw tells of the death of his father who had been to visit an old friend, Major Freebody, who was in command of one of the forts upon Portsdown Hill. The unfortunate man, while returning to the fort in the twilight, fell into one of the chalk pits, fracturing his skull with fatal results.*

During the dark days of the war many Portsmouth people took refuge beneath the chalk of the hill in either the London Road shelter or the Wymering shelter. Entrance to both refuges was by ticket and shelter dwellers would have slept in these three-tier bunks, which were common to both shelters.

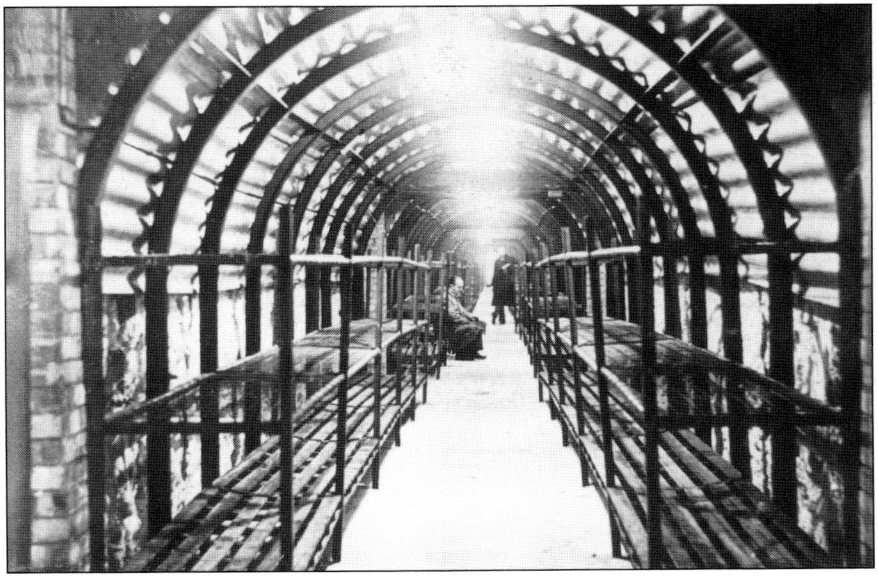

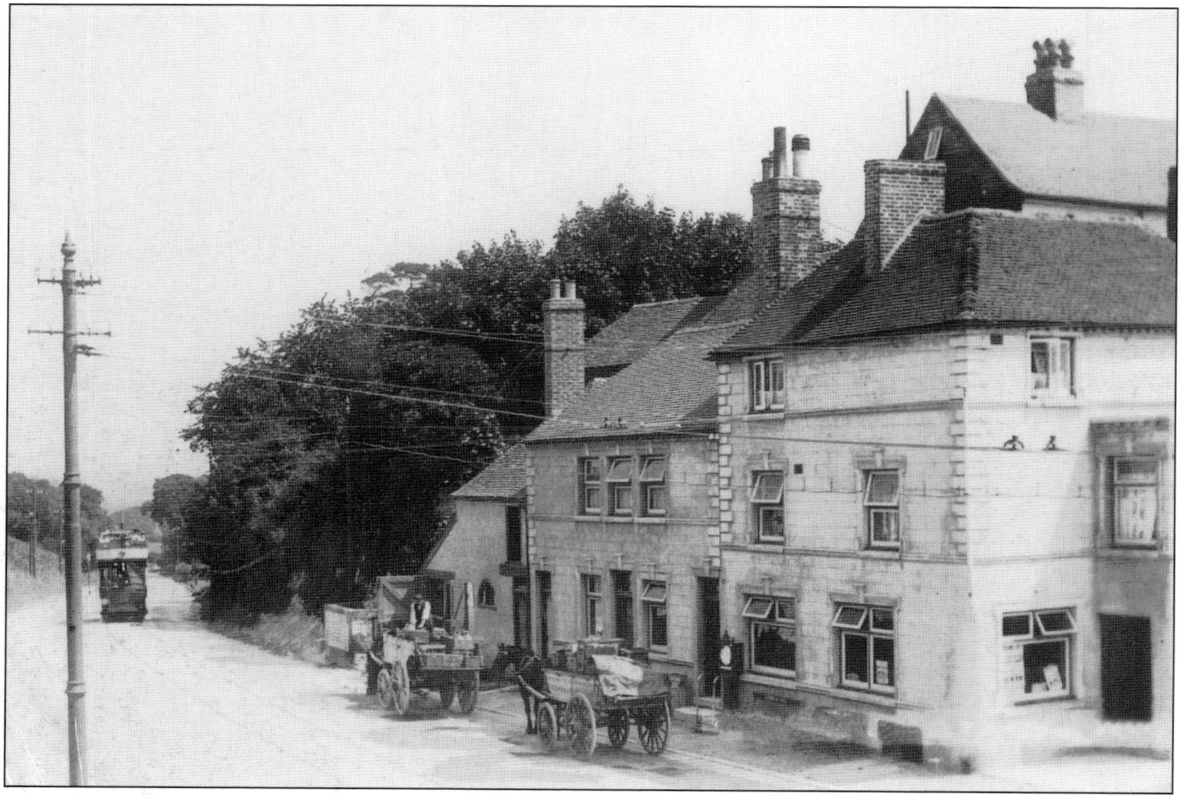

Above: *The George Inn crossroads must have seen a panorama of history throughout the years – famous people, sailors travelling to and from Portsmouth, and probably a few highwaymen! A tram is making its way from Horndean, passing close to two examples of an earlier mode of transport.*

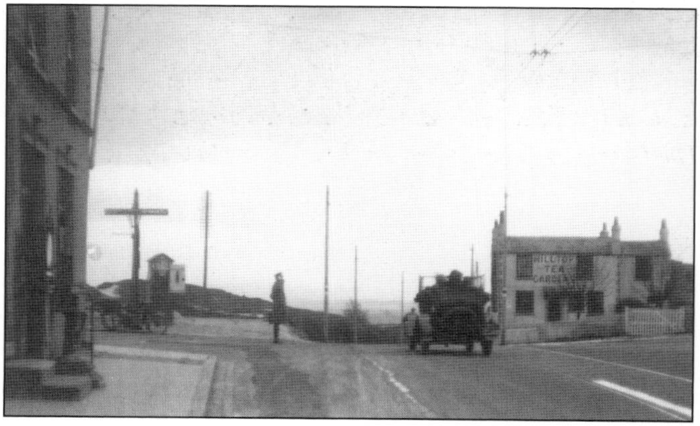

Right: *The George is on the left of this picture from the early days of motoring. The RAC officer has left his motorcycle near the organisation's phone box to salute a passing car, while he keeps a weather eye on the traffic.*

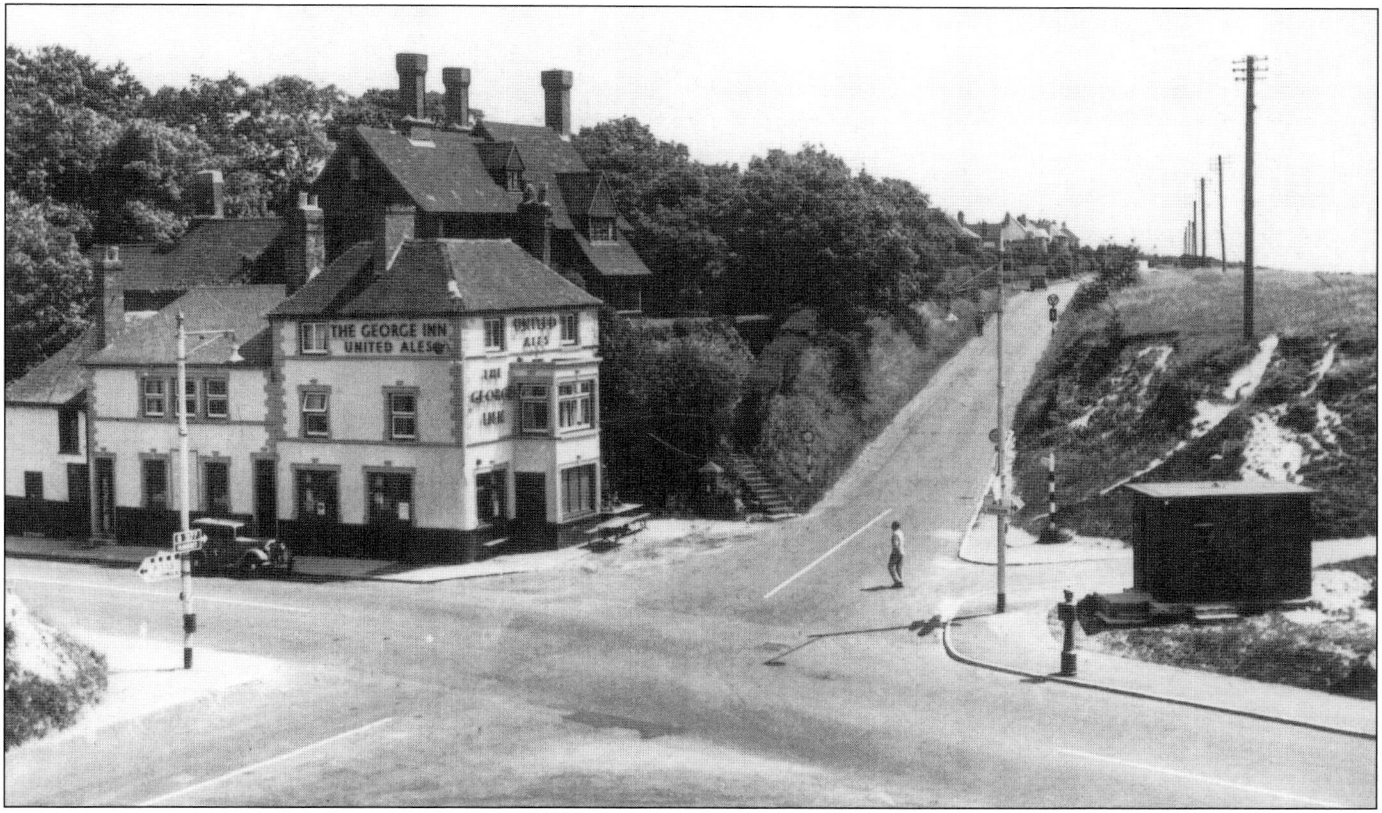

The George is pictured here in those balmy days between the wars, with only two cars in sight at this present-day busy junction.

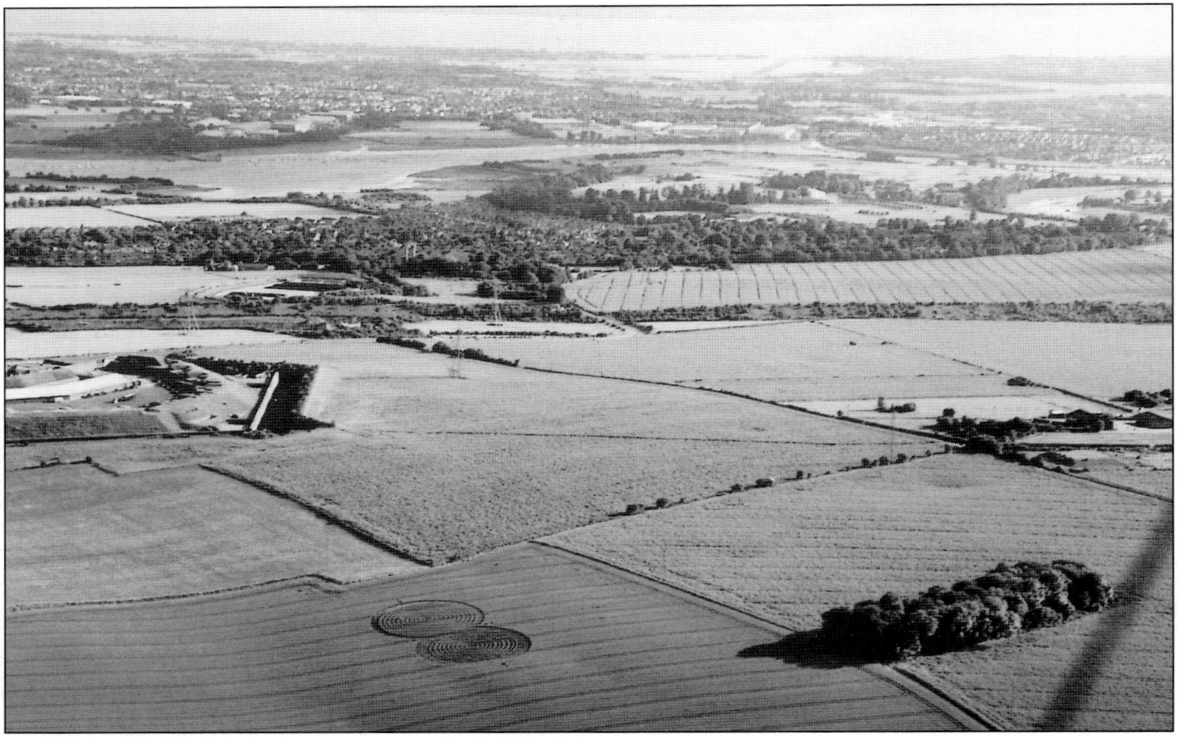

Above: *The final pictures in this collection take the reader into the future – or is it the past? Fort Nelson is seen centre left of this stunning picture of a superb example of the crop circle phenomenon set on the slopes of Portsdown Hill. This image was taken in June 2004 by – and is reproduced here by permission of – crop circle expert, author and photographer Lucy Pringle. The close-up shot* (right) *shows perfectly the complex double spiral shape, with one half being a negative of the other. The strange appearance of crop circles has certainly prompted many schools of thought. Are they communications from extra-terrestrials, or are they evidence of another dimension? Whatever the answer, this picture nevertheless makes an unusual end to this look at Portsdown.*

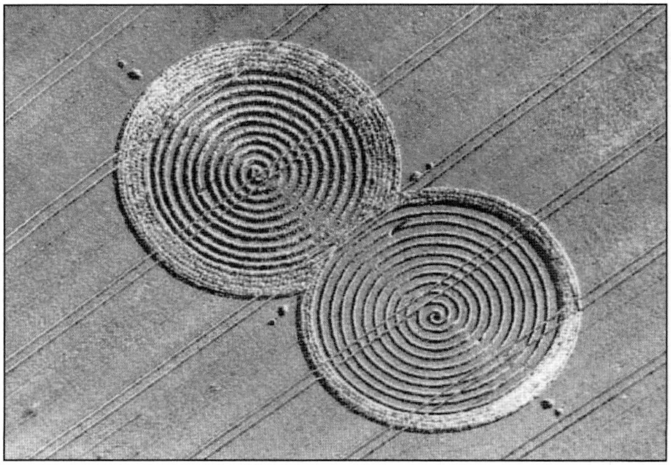